C-1825   CAREER EXAMINATION SERIES

This is your
PASSBOOK for...

Head Custodian III

Test Preparation Study Guide
Questions & Answers

NATIONAL LEARNING CORPORATION®

COPYRIGHT NOTICE

This book is SOLELY intended for, is sold ONLY to, and its use is RESTRICTED to individual, bona fide applicants or candidates who qualify by virtue of having seriously filed applications for appropriate license, certificate, professional and/or promotional advancement, higher school matriculation, scholarship, or other legitimate requirements of education and/or governmental authorities.

This book is NOT intended for use, class instruction, tutoring, training, duplication, copying, reprinting, excerption, or adaptation, etc., by:

1) Other publishers
2) Proprietors and/or Instructors of "Coaching" and/or Preparatory Courses
3) Personnel and/or Training Divisions of commercial, industrial, and governmental organizations
4) Schools, colleges, or universities and/or their departments and staffs, including teachers and other personnel
5) Testing Agencies or Bureaus
6) Study groups which seek by the purchase of a single volume to copy and/or duplicate and/or adapt this material for use by the group as a whole without having purchased individual volumes for each of the members of the group
7) Et al.

Such persons would be in violation of appropriate Federal and State statutes.

PROVISION OF LICENSING AGREEMENTS – Recognized educational, commercial, industrial, and governmental institutions and organizations, and others legitimately engaged in educational pursuits, including training, testing, and measurement activities, may address request for a licensing agreement to the copyright owners, who will determine whether, and under what conditions, including fees and charges, the materials in this book may be used them. In other words, a licensing facility exists for the legitimate use of the material in this book on other than an individual basis. However, it is asseverated and affirmed here that the material in this book CANNOT be used without the receipt of the express permission of such a licensing agreement from the Publishers. Inquiries re licensing should be addressed to the company, attention rights and permissions department.

All rights reserved, including the right of reproduction in whole or in part, in any form or by any means, electronic or mechanical, including photocopying, recording, or by any information storage and retrieval system, without permission in writing from the Publisher.

Copyright © 2024 by
National Learning Corporation

212 Michael Drive, Syosset, NY 11791
(516) 921-8888 • www.passbooks.com
E-mail: info@passbooks.com

PUBLISHED IN THE UNITED STATES OF AMERICA

PASSBOOK® SERIES

THE *PASSBOOK® SERIES* has been created to prepare applicants and candidates for the ultimate academic battlefield – the examination room.

At some time in our lives, each and every one of us may be required to take an examination – for validation, matriculation, admission, qualification, registration, certification, or licensure.

Based on the assumption that every applicant or candidate has met the basic formal educational standards, has taken the required number of courses, and read the necessary texts, the *PASSBOOK® SERIES* furnishes the one special preparation which may assure passing with confidence, instead of failing with insecurity. Examination questions – together with answers – are furnished as the basic vehicle for study so that the mysteries of the examination and its compounding difficulties may be eliminated or diminished by a sure method.

This book is meant to help you pass your examination provided that you qualify and are serious in your objective.

The entire field is reviewed through the huge store of content information which is succinctly presented through a provocative and challenging approach – the question-and-answer method.

A climate of success is established by furnishing the correct answers at the end of each test.

You soon learn to recognize types of questions, forms of questions, and patterns of questioning. You may even begin to anticipate expected outcomes.

You perceive that many questions are repeated or adapted so that you can gain acute insights, which may enable you to score many sure points.

You learn how to confront new questions, or types of questions, and to attack them confidently and work out the correct answers.

You note objectives and emphases, and recognize pitfalls and dangers, so that you may make positive educational adjustments.

Moreover, you are kept fully informed in relation to new concepts, methods, practices, and directions in the field.

You discover that you are actually taking the examination all the time: you are preparing for the examination by "taking" an examination, not by reading extraneous and/or supererogatory textbooks.

In short, this PASSBOOK®, used directedly, should be an important factor in helping you to pass your test.

HEAD CUSTODIAN III

DUTIES:
Supervises the cleaning of classrooms and other areas in a school building; orders, stores and issues cleaning supplies; trains newly assigned custodial workers in their duties. Operates and performs maintenance work on electrical, plumbing, heating and ventilating systems including low and high pressure steam boilers and oil burners. Maintains necessary records and prepares required reports relating to personnel, supplies, equipment and work performed. Supervises subordinate Head Custodians I and II. Does related work as required.

SCOPE OF THE EXAMINATION:
The written test is designed to evaluate knowledge, skills and/or abilities in such areas as:
1. **Ability to read and follow written instructions** - These questions test for the ability to read, understand and apply written instructions for performing tasks similar to those encountered on the job. All the information needed to answer these questions will be provided in the test booklet.
2. **Building cleaning** - These questions test for knowledge of basic principles and practices of building cleaning. They cover such areas as equipment, tools, supplies, methods and procedures for cleaning different types of surfaces and materials under various, commonly occurring circumstances.
3. **Building operation and maintenance I** - These questions test for knowledge of the basic principles, practices and techniques essential to the correct operation and maintenance of public buildings. They cover such areas as building maintenance; preventive maintenance, and minor repair of electrical and plumbing systems; methods and equipment for snow removal; building safety and equipment storage.
4. **Operation and routine maintenance of heating, ventilating and air conditioning systems** - These questions test for knowledge of basic principles, practices and techniques essential to the correct operation and maintenance of heating, ventilating and air conditioning systems, including such areas as minor cleaning; room temperature and building ventilation control; steam, hot water and hot air heating systems; boiler operation; troubleshooting air conditioning system problems, and proper maintenance of air conditioning systems.
5. **Supervision and training** - These questions test for the knowledge required by a supervisor to set goals, plan and organize work, train workers in how to do their jobs, and direct workers towards meeting established goals. The supervisory questions cover such areas as assigning and reviewing work, evaluating performance, maintaining work quality, motivating employees, increasing efficiency, and dealing with problems that may arise on the job. The training questions cover such areas as determining the necessity for training, selecting appropriate training methods, and evaluating the effectiveness of training.

HOW TO TAKE A TEST

I. YOU MUST PASS AN EXAMINATION

A. WHAT EVERY CANDIDATE SHOULD KNOW

Examination applicants often ask us for help in preparing for the written test. What can I study in advance? What kinds of questions will be asked? How will the test be given? How will the papers be graded?

As an applicant for a civil service examination, you may be wondering about some of these things. Our purpose here is to suggest effective methods of advance study and to describe civil service examinations.

Your chances for success on this examination can be increased if you know how to prepare. Those "pre-examination jitters" can be reduced if you know what to expect. You can even experience an adventure in good citizenship if you know why civil service exams are given.

B. WHY ARE CIVIL SERVICE EXAMINATIONS GIVEN?

Civil service examinations are important to you in two ways. As a citizen, you want public jobs filled by employees who know how to do their work. As a job seeker, you want a fair chance to compete for that job on an equal footing with other candidates. The best-known means of accomplishing this two-fold goal is the competitive examination.

Exams are widely publicized throughout the nation. They may be administered for jobs in federal, state, city, municipal, town or village governments or agencies.

Any citizen may apply, with some limitations, such as the age or residence of applicants. Your experience and education may be reviewed to see whether you meet the requirements for the particular examination. When these requirements exist, they are reasonable and applied consistently to all applicants. Thus, a competitive examination may cause you some uneasiness now, but it is your privilege and safeguard.

C. HOW ARE CIVIL SERVICE EXAMS DEVELOPED?

Examinations are carefully written by trained technicians who are specialists in the field known as "psychological measurement," in consultation with recognized authorities in the field of work that the test will cover. These experts recommend the subject matter areas or skills to be tested; only those knowledges or skills important to your success on the job are included. The most reliable books and source materials available are used as references. Together, the experts and technicians judge the difficulty level of the questions.

Test technicians know how to phrase questions so that the problem is clearly stated. Their ethics do not permit "trick" or "catch" questions. Questions may have been tried out on sample groups, or subjected to statistical analysis, to determine their usefulness.

Written tests are often used in combination with performance tests, ratings of training and experience, and oral interviews. All of these measures combine to form the best-known means of finding the right person for the right job.

II. HOW TO PASS THE WRITTEN TEST

A. NATURE OF THE EXAMINATION

To prepare intelligently for civil service examinations, you should know how they differ from school examinations you have taken. In school you were assigned certain definite pages to read or subjects to cover. The examination questions were quite detailed and usually emphasized memory. Civil service exams, on the other hand, try to discover your present ability to perform the duties of a position, plus your potentiality to learn these duties. In other words, a civil service exam attempts to predict how successful you will be. Questions cover such a broad area that they cannot be as minute and detailed as school exam questions.

In the public service similar kinds of work, or positions, are grouped together in one "class." This process is known as *position-classification*. All the positions in a class are paid according to the salary range for that class. One class title covers all of these positions, and they are all tested by the same examination.

B. FOUR BASIC STEPS

1) Study the announcement

How, then, can you know what subjects to study? Our best answer is: "Learn as much as possible about the class of positions for which you've applied." The exam will test the knowledge, skills and abilities needed to do the work.

Your most valuable source of information about the position you want is the official exam announcement. This announcement lists the training and experience qualifications. Check these standards and apply only if you come reasonably close to meeting them.

The brief description of the position in the examination announcement offers some clues to the subjects which will be tested. Think about the job itself. Review the duties in your mind. Can you perform them, or are there some in which you are rusty? Fill in the blank spots in your preparation.

Many jurisdictions preview the written test in the exam announcement by including a section called "Knowledge and Abilities Required," "Scope of the Examination," or some similar heading. Here you will find out specifically what fields will be tested.

2) Review your own background

Once you learn in general what the position is all about, and what you need to know to do the work, ask yourself which subjects you already know fairly well and which need improvement. You may wonder whether to concentrate on improving your strong areas or on building some background in your fields of weakness. When the announcement has specified "some knowledge" or "considerable knowledge," or has used adjectives like "beginning principles of..." or "advanced ... methods," you can get a clue as to the number and difficulty of questions to be asked in any given field. More questions, and hence broader coverage, would be included for those subjects which are more important in the work. Now weigh your strengths and weaknesses against the job requirements and prepare accordingly.

3) Determine the level of the position

Another way to tell how intensively you should prepare is to understand the level of the job for which you are applying. Is it the entering level? In other words, is this the position in which beginners in a field of work are hired? Or is it an intermediate or advanced level? Sometimes this is indicated by such words as "Junior" or "Senior" in the class title. Other jurisdictions use Roman numerals to designate the level – Clerk I, Clerk II, for example. The word "Supervisor" sometimes appears in the title. If the level is not indicated by the title, check the description of duties. Will you be working under very close supervision, or will you have responsibility for independent decisions in this work?

4) Choose appropriate study materials

Now that you know the subjects to be examined and the relative amount of each subject to be covered, you can choose suitable study materials. For beginning level jobs, or even advanced ones, if you have a pronounced weakness in some aspect of your training, read a modern, standard textbook in that field. Be sure it is up to date and has general coverage. Such books are normally available at your library, and the librarian will be glad to help you locate one. For entry-level positions, questions of appropriate difficulty are chosen – neither highly advanced questions, nor those too simple. Such questions require careful thought but not advanced training.

If the position for which you are applying is technical or advanced, you will read more advanced, specialized material. If you are already familiar with the basic principles of your field, elementary textbooks would waste your time. Concentrate on advanced textbooks and technical periodicals. Think through the concepts and review difficult problems in your field.

These are all general sources. You can get more ideas on your own initiative, following these leads. For example, training manuals and publications of the government agency which employs workers in your field can be useful, particularly for technical and professional positions. A letter or visit to the government department involved may result in more specific study suggestions, and certainly will provide you with a more definite idea of the exact nature of the position you are seeking.

III. KINDS OF TESTS

Tests are used for purposes other than measuring knowledge and ability to perform specified duties. For some positions, it is equally important to test ability to make adjustments to new situations or to profit from training. In others, basic mental abilities not dependent on information are essential. Questions which test these things may not appear as pertinent to the duties of the position as those which test for knowledge and information. Yet they are often highly important parts of a fair examination. For very general questions, it is almost impossible to help you direct your study efforts. What we can do is to point out some of the more common of these general abilities needed in public service positions and describe some typical questions.

1) General information

Broad, general information has been found useful for predicting job success in some kinds of work. This is tested in a variety of ways, from vocabulary lists to questions about current events. Basic background in some field of work, such as sociology or economics, may be sampled in a group of questions. Often these are principles which have become familiar to most persons through exposure rather than through formal training. It is difficult to advise you how to study for these questions; being alert to the world around you is our best suggestion.

2) Verbal ability

An example of an ability needed in many positions is verbal or language ability. Verbal ability is, in brief, the ability to use and understand words. Vocabulary and grammar tests are typical measures of this ability. Reading comprehension or paragraph interpretation questions are common in many kinds of civil service tests. You are given a paragraph of written material and asked to find its central meaning.

3) Numerical ability

Number skills can be tested by the familiar arithmetic problem, by checking paired lists of numbers to see which are alike and which are different, or by interpreting charts and graphs. In the latter test, a graph may be printed in the test booklet which you are asked to use as the basis for answering questions.

4) Observation

A popular test for law-enforcement positions is the observation test. A picture is shown to you for several minutes, then taken away. Questions about the picture test your ability to observe both details and larger elements.

5) Following directions

In many positions in the public service, the employee must be able to carry out written instructions dependably and accurately. You may be given a chart with several columns, each column listing a variety of information. The questions require you to carry out directions involving the information given in the chart.

6) Skills and aptitudes

Performance tests effectively measure some manual skills and aptitudes. When the skill is one in which you are trained, such as typing or shorthand, you can practice. These tests are often very much like those given in business school or high school courses. For many of the other skills and aptitudes, however, no short-time preparation can be made. Skills and abilities natural to you or that you have developed throughout your lifetime are being tested.

Many of the general questions just described provide all the data needed to answer the questions and ask you to use your reasoning ability to find the answers. Your best preparation for these tests, as well as for tests of facts and ideas, is to be at your physical and mental best. You, no doubt, have your own methods of getting into an exam-taking mood and keeping "in shape." The next section lists some ideas on this subject.

IV. KINDS OF QUESTIONS

Only rarely is the "essay" question, which you answer in narrative form, used in civil service tests. Civil service tests are usually of the short-answer type. Full instructions for answering these questions will be given to you at the examination. But in case this is your first experience with short-answer questions and separate answer sheets, here is what you need to know:

1) Multiple-choice Questions

Most popular of the short-answer questions is the "multiple choice" or "best answer" question. It can be used, for example, to test for factual knowledge, ability to solve problems or judgment in meeting situations found at work.

A multiple-choice question is normally one of three types—
- It can begin with an incomplete statement followed by several possible endings. You are to find the one ending which *best* completes the statement, although some of the others may not be entirely wrong.
- It can also be a complete statement in the form of a question which is answered by choosing one of the statements listed.

- It can be in the form of a problem – again you select the best answer.

Here is an example of a multiple-choice question with a discussion which should give you some clues as to the method for choosing the right answer:

When an employee has a complaint about his assignment, the action which will *best* help him overcome his difficulty is to
    A. discuss his difficulty with his coworkers
    B. take the problem to the head of the organization
    C. take the problem to the person who gave him the assignment
    D. say nothing to anyone about his complaint

In answering this question, you should study each of the choices to find which is best. Consider choice "A" – Certainly an employee may discuss his complaint with fellow employees, but no change or improvement can result, and the complaint remains unresolved. Choice "B" is a poor choice since the head of the organization probably does not know what assignment you have been given, and taking your problem to him is known as "going over the head" of the supervisor. The supervisor, or person who made the assignment, is the person who can clarify it or correct any injustice. Choice "C" is, therefore, correct. To say nothing, as in choice "D," is unwise. Supervisors have and interest in knowing the problems employees are facing, and the employee is seeking a solution to his problem.

2) True/False Questions

The "true/false" or "right/wrong" form of question is sometimes used. Here a complete statement is given. Your job is to decide whether the statement is right or wrong.

SAMPLE: A roaming cell-phone call to a nearby city costs less than a non-roaming call to a distant city.

This statement is wrong, or false, since roaming calls are more expensive.

This is not a complete list of all possible question forms, although most of the others are variations of these common types. You will always get complete directions for answering questions. Be sure you understand *how* to mark your answers – ask questions until you do.

V. RECORDING YOUR ANSWERS

Computer terminals are used more and more today for many different kinds of exams.

For an examination with very few applicants, you may be told to record your answers in the test booklet itself. Separate answer sheets are much more common. If this separate answer sheet is to be scored by machine – and this is often the case – it is highly important that you mark your answers correctly in order to get credit.

An electronic scoring machine is often used in civil service offices because of the speed with which papers can be scored. Machine-scored answer sheets must be marked with a pencil, which will be given to you. This pencil has a high graphite content which responds to the electronic scoring machine. As a matter of fact, stray dots may register as answers, so do not let your pencil rest on the answer sheet while you are pondering the correct answer. Also, if your pencil lead breaks or is otherwise defective, ask for another.

Since the answer sheet will be dropped in a slot in the scoring machine, be careful not to bend the corners or get the paper crumpled.

The answer sheet normally has five vertical columns of numbers, with 30 numbers to a column. These numbers correspond to the question numbers in your test booklet. After each number, going across the page are four or five pairs of dotted lines. These short dotted lines have small letters or numbers above them. The first two pairs may also have a "T" or "F" above the letters. This indicates that the first two pairs only are to be used if the questions are of the true-false type. If the questions are multiple choice, disregard the "T" and "F" and pay attention only to the small letters or numbers.

Answer your questions in the manner of the sample that follows:

32. The largest city in the United States is
    A. Washington, D.C.
    B. New York City
    C. Chicago
    D. Detroit
    E. San Francisco

1) Choose the answer you think is best. (New York City is the largest, so "B" is correct.)
2) Find the row of dotted lines numbered the same as the question you are answering. (Find row number 32)
3) Find the pair of dotted lines corresponding to the answer. (Find the pair of lines under the mark "B.")
4) Make a solid black mark between the dotted lines.

VI. BEFORE THE TEST

Common sense will help you find procedures to follow to get ready for an examination. Too many of us, however, overlook these sensible measures. Indeed, nervousness and fatigue have been found to be the most serious reasons why applicants fail to do their best on civil service tests. Here is a list of reminders:

- Begin your preparation early – Don't wait until the last minute to go scurrying around for books and materials or to find out what the position is all about.
- Prepare continuously – An hour a night for a week is better than an all-night cram session. This has been definitely established. What is more, a night a week for a month will return better dividends than crowding your study into a shorter period of time.
- Locate the place of the exam – You have been sent a notice telling you when and where to report for the examination. If the location is in a different town or otherwise unfamiliar to you, it would be well to inquire the best route and learn something about the building.
- Relax the night before the test – Allow your mind to rest. Do not study at all that night. Plan some mild recreation or diversion; then go to bed early and get a good night's sleep.
- Get up early enough to make a leisurely trip to the place for the test – This way unforeseen events, traffic snarls, unfamiliar buildings, etc. will not upset you.
- Dress comfortably – A written test is not a fashion show. You will be known by number and not by name, so wear something comfortable.

- Leave excess paraphernalia at home – Shopping bags and odd bundles will get in your way. You need bring only the items mentioned in the official notice you received; usually everything you need is provided. Do not bring reference books to the exam. They will only confuse those last minutes and be taken away from you when in the test room.
- Arrive somewhat ahead of time – If because of transportation schedules you must get there very early, bring a newspaper or magazine to take your mind off yourself while waiting.
- Locate the examination room – When you have found the proper room, you will be directed to the seat or part of the room where you will sit. Sometimes you are given a sheet of instructions to read while you are waiting. Do not fill out any forms until you are told to do so; just read them and be prepared.
- Relax and prepare to listen to the instructions
- If you have any physical problem that may keep you from doing your best, be sure to tell the test administrator. If you are sick or in poor health, you really cannot do your best on the exam. You can come back and take the test some other time.

VII. AT THE TEST

The day of the test is here and you have the test booklet in your hand. The temptation to get going is very strong. Caution! There is more to success than knowing the right answers. You must know how to identify your papers and understand variations in the type of short-answer question used in this particular examination. Follow these suggestions for maximum results from your efforts:

1) Cooperate with the monitor

The test administrator has a duty to create a situation in which you can be as much at ease as possible. He will give instructions, tell you when to begin, check to see that you are marking your answer sheet correctly, and so on. He is not there to guard you, although he will see that your competitors do not take unfair advantage. He wants to help you do your best.

2) Listen to all instructions

Don't jump the gun! Wait until you understand all directions. In most civil service tests you get more time than you need to answer the questions. So don't be in a hurry. Read each word of instructions until you clearly understand the meaning. Study the examples, listen to all announcements and follow directions. Ask questions if you do not understand what to do.

3) Identify your papers

Civil service exams are usually identified by number only. You will be assigned a number; you must not put your name on your test papers. Be sure to copy your number correctly. Since more than one exam may be given, copy your exact examination title.

4) Plan your time

Unless you are told that a test is a "speed" or "rate of work" test, speed itself is usually not important. Time enough to answer all the questions will be provided, but this does not mean that you have all day. An overall time limit has been set. Divide the total time (in minutes) by the number of questions to determine the approximate time you have for each question.

5) Do not linger over difficult questions

If you come across a difficult question, mark it with a paper clip (useful to have along) and come back to it when you have been through the booklet. One caution if you do this – be sure to skip a number on your answer sheet as well. Check often to be sure that you have not lost your place and that you are marking in the row numbered the same as the question you are answering.

6) Read the questions

Be sure you know what the question asks! Many capable people are unsuccessful because they failed to *read* the questions correctly.

7) Answer all questions

Unless you have been instructed that a penalty will be deducted for incorrect answers, it is better to guess than to omit a question.

8) Speed tests

It is often better NOT to guess on speed tests. It has been found that on timed tests people are tempted to spend the last few seconds before time is called in marking answers at random – without even reading them – in the hope of picking up a few extra points. To discourage this practice, the instructions may warn you that your score will be "corrected" for guessing. That is, a penalty will be applied. The incorrect answers will be deducted from the correct ones, or some other penalty formula will be used.

9) Review your answers

If you finish before time is called, go back to the questions you guessed or omitted to give them further thought. Review other answers if you have time.

10) Return your test materials

If you are ready to leave before others have finished or time is called, take ALL your materials to the monitor and leave quietly. Never take any test material with you. The monitor can discover whose papers are not complete, and taking a test booklet may be grounds for disqualification.

VIII. EXAMINATION TECHNIQUES

1) Read the general instructions carefully. These are usually printed on the first page of the exam booklet. As a rule, these instructions refer to the timing of the examination; the fact that you should not start work until the signal and must stop work at a signal, etc. If there are any *special* instructions, such as a choice of questions to be answered, make sure that you note this instruction carefully.

2) When you are ready to start work on the examination, that is as soon as the signal has been given, read the instructions to each question booklet, underline any key words or phrases, such as *least, best, outline, describe* and the like. In this way you will tend to answer as requested rather than discover on reviewing your paper that you *listed without describing*, that you selected the *worst* choice rather than the *best* choice, etc.

3) If the examination is of the objective or multiple-choice type – that is, each question will also give a series of possible answers: A, B, C or D, and you are called upon to select the best answer and write the letter next to that answer on your answer paper – it is advisable to start answering each question in turn. There may be anywhere from 50 to 100 such questions in the three or four hours allotted and you can see how much time would be taken if you read through all the questions before beginning to answer any. Furthermore, if you come across a question or group of questions which you know would be difficult to answer, it would undoubtedly affect your handling of all the other questions.

4) If the examination is of the essay type and contains but a few questions, it is a moot point as to whether you should read all the questions before starting to answer any one. Of course, if you are given a choice – say five out of seven and the like – then it is essential to read all the questions so you can eliminate the two that are most difficult. If, however, you are asked to answer all the questions, there may be danger in trying to answer the easiest one first because you may find that you will spend too much time on it. The best technique is to answer the first question, then proceed to the second, etc.

5) Time your answers. Before the exam begins, write down the time it started, then add the time allowed for the examination and write down the time it must be completed, then divide the time available somewhat as follows:
    - If 3-1/2 hours are allowed, that would be 210 minutes. If you have 80 objective-type questions, that would be an average of 2-1/2 minutes per question. Allow yourself no more than 2 minutes per question, or a total of 160 minutes, which will permit about 50 minutes to review.
    - If for the time allotment of 210 minutes there are 7 essay questions to answer, that would average about 30 minutes a question. Give yourself only 25 minutes per question so that you have about 35 minutes to review.

6) The most important instruction is to *read each question* and make sure you know what is wanted. The second most important instruction is to *time yourself properly* so that you answer every question. The third most important instruction is to *answer every question*. Guess if you have to but include something for each question. Remember that you will receive no credit for a blank and will probably receive some credit if you write something in answer to an essay question. If you guess a letter – say "B" for a multiple-choice question – you may have guessed right. If you leave a blank as an answer to a multiple-choice question, the examiners may respect your feelings but it will not add a point to your score. Some exams may penalize you for wrong answers, so in such cases *only*, you may not want to guess unless you have some basis for your answer.

7) Suggestions
    a. Objective-type questions
        1. Examine the question booklet for proper sequence of pages and questions
        2. Read all instructions carefully
        3. Skip any question which seems too difficult; return to it after all other questions have been answered
        4. Apportion your time properly; do not spend too much time on any single question or group of questions

5. Note and underline key words – *all, most, fewest, least, best, worst, same, opposite*, etc.
6. Pay particular attention to negatives
7. Note unusual option, e.g., unduly long, short, complex, different or similar in content to the body of the question
8. Observe the use of "hedging" words – *probably, may, most likely*, etc.
9. Make sure that your answer is put next to the same number as the question
10. Do not second-guess unless you have good reason to believe the second answer is definitely more correct
11. Cross out original answer if you decide another answer is more accurate; do not erase until you are ready to hand your paper in
12. Answer all questions; guess unless instructed otherwise
13. Leave time for review

  b. Essay questions
    1. Read each question carefully
    2. Determine exactly what is wanted. Underline key words or phrases.
    3. Decide on outline or paragraph answer
    4. Include many different points and elements unless asked to develop any one or two points or elements
    5. Show impartiality by giving pros and cons unless directed to select one side only
    6. Make and write down any assumptions you find necessary to answer the questions
    7. Watch your English, grammar, punctuation and choice of words
    8. Time your answers; don't crowd material

8) Answering the essay question

Most essay questions can be answered by framing the specific response around several key words or ideas. Here are a few such key words or ideas:

M's: manpower, materials, methods, money, management
P's: purpose, program, policy, plan, procedure, practice, problems, pitfalls, personnel, public relations

  a. Six basic steps in handling problems:
    1. Preliminary plan and background development
    2. Collect information, data and facts
    3. Analyze and interpret information, data and facts
    4. Analyze and develop solutions as well as make recommendations
    5. Prepare report and sell recommendations
    6. Install recommendations and follow up effectiveness

  b. Pitfalls to avoid
    1. *Taking things for granted* – A statement of the situation does not necessarily imply that each of the elements is necessarily true; for example, a complaint may be invalid and biased so that all that can be taken for granted is that a complaint has been registered

2. *Considering only one side of a situation* – Wherever possible, indicate several alternatives and then point out the reasons you selected the best one
3. *Failing to indicate follow up* – Whenever your answer indicates action on your part, make certain that you will take proper follow-up action to see how successful your recommendations, procedures or actions turn out to be
4. *Taking too long in answering any single question* – Remember to time your answers properly

IX. AFTER THE TEST

Scoring procedures differ in detail among civil service jurisdictions although the general principles are the same. Whether the papers are hand-scored or graded by machine we have described, they are nearly always graded by number. That is, the person who marks the paper knows only the number – never the name – of the applicant. Not until all the papers have been graded will they be matched with names. If other tests, such as training and experience or oral interview ratings have been given, scores will be combined. Different parts of the examination usually have different weights. For example, the written test might count 60 percent of the final grade, and a rating of training and experience 40 percent. In many jurisdictions, veterans will have a certain number of points added to their grades.

After the final grade has been determined, the names are placed in grade order and an eligible list is established. There are various methods for resolving ties between those who get the same final grade – probably the most common is to place first the name of the person whose application was received first. Job offers are made from the eligible list in the order the names appear on it. You will be notified of your grade and your rank as soon as all these computations have been made. This will be done as rapidly as possible.

People who are found to meet the requirements in the announcement are called "eligibles." Their names are put on a list of eligible candidates. An eligible's chances of getting a job depend on how high he stands on this list and how fast agencies are filling jobs from the list.

When a job is to be filled from a list of eligibles, the agency asks for the names of people on the list of eligibles for that job. When the civil service commission receives this request, it sends to the agency the names of the three people highest on this list. Or, if the job to be filled has specialized requirements, the office sends the agency the names of the top three persons who meet these requirements from the general list.

The appointing officer makes a choice from among the three people whose names were sent to him. If the selected person accepts the appointment, the names of the others are put back on the list to be considered for future openings.

That is the rule in hiring from all kinds of eligible lists, whether they are for typist, carpenter, chemist, or something else. For every vacancy, the appointing officer has his choice of any one of the top three eligibles on the list. This explains why the person whose name is on top of the list sometimes does not get an appointment when some of the persons lower on the list do. If the appointing officer chooses the second or third eligible, the No. 1 eligible does not get a job at once, but stays on the list until he is appointed or the list is terminated.

X. HOW TO PASS THE INTERVIEW TEST

The examination for which you applied requires an oral interview test. You have already taken the written test and you are now being called for the interview test – the final part of the formal examination.

You may think that it is not possible to prepare for an interview test and that there are no procedures to follow during an interview. Our purpose is to point out some things you can do in advance that will help you and some good rules to follow and pitfalls to avoid while you are being interviewed.

What is an interview supposed to test?

The written examination is designed to test the technical knowledge and competence of the candidate; the oral is designed to evaluate intangible qualities, not readily measured otherwise, and to establish a list showing the relative fitness of each candidate – as measured against his competitors – for the position sought. Scoring is not on the basis of "right" and "wrong," but on a sliding scale of values ranging from "not passable" to "outstanding." As a matter of fact, it is possible to achieve a relatively low score without a single "incorrect" answer because of evident weakness in the qualities being measured.

Occasionally, an examination may consist entirely of an oral test – either an individual or a group oral. In such cases, information is sought concerning the technical knowledges and abilities of the candidate, since there has been no written examination for this purpose. More commonly, however, an oral test is used to supplement a written examination.

Who conducts interviews?

The composition of oral boards varies among different jurisdictions. In nearly all, a representative of the personnel department serves as chairman. One of the members of the board may be a representative of the department in which the candidate would work. In some cases, "outside experts" are used, and, frequently, a businessman or some other representative of the general public is asked to serve. Labor and management or other special groups may be represented. The aim is to secure the services of experts in the appropriate field.

However the board is composed, it is a good idea (and not at all improper or unethical) to ascertain in advance of the interview who the members are and what groups they represent. When you are introduced to them, you will have some idea of their backgrounds and interests, and at least you will not stutter and stammer over their names.

What should be done before the interview?

While knowledge about the board members is useful and takes some of the surprise element out of the interview, there is other preparation which is more substantive. It *is* possible to prepare for an oral interview – in several ways:

1) Keep a copy of your application and review it carefully before the interview

This may be the only document before the oral board, and the starting point of the interview. Know what education and experience you have listed there, and the sequence and dates of all of it. Sometimes the board will ask you to review the highlights of your experience for them; you should not have to hem and haw doing it.

2) Study the class specification and the examination announcement

Usually, the oral board has one or both of these to guide them. The qualities, characteristics or knowledges required by the position sought are stated in these documents. They offer valuable clues as to the nature of the oral interview. For example, if the job involves supervisory responsibilities, the announcement will usually indicate that knowledge of modern supervisory methods and the qualifications of the candidate as a supervisor will be tested. If so, you can expect such questions, frequently in the form of a hypothetical situation which you are expected to solve. NEVER go into an oral without knowledge of the duties and responsibilities of the job you seek.

3) Think through each qualification required

Try to visualize the kind of questions you would ask if you were a board member. How well could you answer them? Try especially to appraise your own knowledge and background in each area, *measured against the job sought*, and identify any areas in which you are weak. Be critical and realistic – do not flatter yourself.

4) Do some general reading in areas in which you feel you may be weak

For example, if the job involves supervision and your past experience has NOT, some general reading in supervisory methods and practices, particularly in the field of human relations, might be useful. Do NOT study agency procedures or detailed manuals. The oral board will be testing your understanding and capacity, not your memory.

5) Get a good night's sleep and watch your general health and mental attitude

You will want a clear head at the interview. Take care of a cold or any other minor ailment, and of course, no hangovers.

What should be done on the day of the interview?

Now comes the day of the interview itself. Give yourself plenty of time to get there. Plan to arrive somewhat ahead of the scheduled time, particularly if your appointment is in the fore part of the day. If a previous candidate fails to appear, the board might be ready for you a bit early. By early afternoon an oral board is almost invariably behind schedule if there are many candidates, and you may have to wait. Take along a book or magazine to read, or your application to review, but leave any extraneous material in the waiting room when you go in for your interview. In any event, relax and compose yourself.

The matter of dress is important. The board is forming impressions about you – from your experience, your manners, your attitude, and your appearance. Give your personal appearance careful attention. Dress your best, but not your flashiest. Choose conservative, appropriate clothing, and be sure it is immaculate. This is a business interview, and your appearance should indicate that you regard it as such. Besides, being well groomed and properly dressed will help boost your confidence.

Sooner or later, someone will call your name and escort you into the interview room. *This is it.* From here on you are on your own. It is too late for any more preparation. But remember, you asked for this opportunity to prove your fitness, and you are here because your request was granted.

What happens when you go in?

The usual sequence of events will be as follows: The clerk (who is often the board stenographer) will introduce you to the chairman of the oral board, who will introduce you to the other members of the board. Acknowledge the introductions before you sit down. Do not be surprised if you find a microphone facing you or a stenotypist sitting by. Oral interviews are usually recorded in the event of an appeal or other review.

Usually the chairman of the board will open the interview by reviewing the highlights of your education and work experience from your application – primarily for the benefit of the other members of the board, as well as to get the material into the record. Do not interrupt or comment unless there is an error or significant misinterpretation; if that is the case, do not hesitate. But do not quibble about insignificant matters. Also, he will usually ask you some question about your education, experience or your present job – partly to get you to start talking and to establish the interviewing "rapport." He may start the actual questioning, or turn it over to one of the other members. Frequently, each member undertakes the questioning on a particular area, one in which he is perhaps most competent, so you can expect each member to participate in the examination. Because time is limited, you may also expect some rather abrupt switches in the direction the questioning takes, so do not be upset by it. Normally, a board member will not pursue a single line of questioning unless he discovers a particular strength or weakness.

After each member has participated, the chairman will usually ask whether any member has any further questions, then will ask you if you have anything you wish to add. Unless you are expecting this question, it may floor you. Worse, it may start you off on an extended, extemporaneous speech. The board is not usually seeking more information. The question is principally to offer you a last opportunity to present further qualifications or to indicate that you have nothing to add. So, if you feel that a significant qualification or characteristic has been overlooked, it is proper to point it out in a sentence or so. Do not compliment the board on the thoroughness of their examination – they have been sketchy, and you know it. If you wish, merely say, "No thank you, I have nothing further to add." This is a point where you can "talk yourself out" of a good impression or fail to present an important bit of information. Remember, *you close the interview yourself*.

The chairman will then say, "That is all, Mr. _____, thank you." Do not be startled; the interview is over, and quicker than you think. Thank him, gather your belongings and take your leave. Save your sigh of relief for the other side of the door.

How to put your best foot forward

Throughout this entire process, you may feel that the board individually and collectively is trying to pierce your defenses, seek out your hidden weaknesses and embarrass and confuse you. Actually, this is not true. They are obliged to make an appraisal of your qualifications for the job you are seeking, and they want to see you in your best light. Remember, they must interview all candidates and a non-cooperative candidate may become a failure in spite of their best efforts to bring out his qualifications. Here are 15 suggestions that will help you:

1) Be natural – Keep your attitude confident, not cocky

If you are not confident that you can do the job, do not expect the board to be. Do not apologize for your weaknesses, try to bring out your strong points. The board is interested in a positive, not negative, presentation. Cockiness will antagonize any board member and make him wonder if you are covering up a weakness by a false show of strength.

2) Get comfortable, but don't lounge or sprawl

Sit erectly but not stiffly. A careless posture may lead the board to conclude that you are careless in other things, or at least that you are not impressed by the importance of the occasion. Either conclusion is natural, even if incorrect. Do not fuss with your clothing, a pencil or an ashtray. Your hands may occasionally be useful to emphasize a point; do not let them become a point of distraction.

3) Do not wisecrack or make small talk

This is a serious situation, and your attitude should show that you consider it as such. Further, the time of the board is limited – they do not want to waste it, and neither should you.

4) Do not exaggerate your experience or abilities
In the first place, from information in the application or other interviews and sources, the board may know more about you than you think. Secondly, you probably will not get away with it. An experienced board is rather adept at spotting such a situation, so do not take the chance.

5) If you know a board member, do not make a point of it, yet do not hide it
Certainly you are not fooling him, and probably not the other members of the board. Do not try to take advantage of your acquaintanceship – it will probably do you little good.

6) Do not dominate the interview
Let the board do that. They will give you the clues – do not assume that you have to do all the talking. Realize that the board has a number of questions to ask you, and do not try to take up all the interview time by showing off your extensive knowledge of the answer to the first one.

7) Be attentive
You only have 20 minutes or so, and you should keep your attention at its sharpest throughout. When a member is addressing a problem or question to you, give him your undivided attention. Address your reply principally to him, but do not exclude the other board members.

8) Do not interrupt
A board member may be stating a problem for you to analyze. He will ask you a question when the time comes. Let him state the problem, and wait for the question.

9) Make sure you understand the question
Do not try to answer until you are sure what the question is. If it is not clear, restate it in your own words or ask the board member to clarify it for you. However, do not haggle about minor elements.

10) Reply promptly but not hastily
A common entry on oral board rating sheets is "candidate responded readily," or "candidate hesitated in replies." Respond as promptly and quickly as you can, but do not jump to a hasty, ill-considered answer.

11) Do not be peremptory in your answers
A brief answer is proper – but do not fire your answer back. That is a losing game from your point of view. The board member can probably ask questions much faster than you can answer them.

12) Do not try to create the answer you think the board member wants
He is interested in what kind of mind you have and how it works – not in playing games. Furthermore, he can usually spot this practice and will actually grade you down on it.

13) Do not switch sides in your reply merely to agree with a board member
Frequently, a member will take a contrary position merely to draw you out and to see if you are willing and able to defend your point of view. Do not start a debate, yet do not surrender a good position. If a position is worth taking, it is worth defending.

14) Do not be afraid to admit an error in judgment if you are shown to be wrong

The board knows that you are forced to reply without any opportunity for careful consideration. Your answer may be demonstrably wrong. If so, admit it and get on with the interview.

15) Do not dwell at length on your present job

The opening question may relate to your present assignment. Answer the question but do not go into an extended discussion. You are being examined for a *new* job, not your present one. As a matter of fact, try to phrase ALL your answers in terms of the job for which you are being examined.

Basis of Rating

Probably you will forget most of these "do's" and "don'ts" when you walk into the oral interview room. Even remembering them all will not ensure you a passing grade. Perhaps you did not have the qualifications in the first place. But remembering them will help you to put your best foot forward, without treading on the toes of the board members.

Rumor and popular opinion to the contrary notwithstanding, an oral board wants you to make the best appearance possible. They know you are under pressure – but they also want to see how you respond to it as a guide to what your reaction would be under the pressures of the job you seek. They will be influenced by the degree of poise you display, the personal traits you show and the manner in which you respond.

ABOUT THIS BOOK

This book contains tests divided into Examination Sections. Go through each test, answering every question in the margin. We have also attached a sample answer sheet at the back of the book that can be removed and used. At the end of each test look at the answer key and check your answers. On the ones you got wrong, look at the right answer choice and learn. Do not fill in the answers first. Do not memorize the questions and answers, but understand the answer and principles involved. On your test, the questions will likely be different from the samples. Questions are changed and new ones added. If you understand these past questions you should have success with any changes that arise. Tests may consist of several types of questions. We have additional books on each subject should more study be advisable or necessary for you. Finally, the more you study, the better prepared you will be. This book is intended to be the last thing you study before you walk into the examination room. Prior study of relevant texts is also recommended. NLC publishes some of these in our Fundamental Series. Knowledge and good sense are important factors in passing your exam. Good luck also helps. So now study this Passbook, absorb the material contained within and take that knowledge into the examination. Then do your best to pass that exam.

EXAMINATION SECTION

EXAMINATION SECTION

TEST 1

DIRECTIONS: Each question or incomplete statement is followed by several suggested answers or completions. Select the one that BEST answers the question or completes the statement. *PRINT THE LETTER OF THE CORRECT ANSWER IN THE SPACE AT THE RIGHT.*

1. An unusually high vacuum reading in a fuel oil suction line may indicate that the
    A. level in the fuel oil tank is low
    B. oil preheater is leaking
    C. oil strainer is dirty
    D. oil is too hot

    1._____

2. The MAIN reason for modulating the flame in a steam heating boiler that has an automatic rotary cup oil burner is to
    A. reduce the number of start and stop operations
    B. guarantee a high-fire start
    C. vary the cut-out pressure
    D. vary the cut-in pressure

    2._____

3. The device on a rotary cup oil burner which senses primary air failure is the
    A. draft sensing device
    B. aquastat
    C. draft alarm
    D. vaporstat

    3._____

4. A 10,000-gallon pressurized house tank contains 8,030 gallons of water, and the pressure gauge reads 60 psi. In the event of a power failure, the number of gallons of water which can be drawn out of the tank before the pressure reading drops to 50 psi is MOST NEARLY
    A. 300   B. 2,000   C. 6,000   D. 8,000

    4._____

5. The heat balancer in a Dunham steam heating system
    A. measures indoor temperatures
    B. controls the firing rate of two or more boilers
    C. measures outdoor temperatures
    D. reacts to the rate of heat output

    5._____

6. In a sub-atmospheric steam heating system, the steam temperature corresponding to a vacuum of 15 inches of mercury is MOST NEARLY _____ °F.
    A. 180   B. 200   C. 212   D. 218

    6._____

7. When the fuel supply to a rotary cup oil burner is cut off, the burner motor switch should open within _____ seconds.
    A. 2   B. 4 to 8   C. 12 to 18   D. 30 to 40

    7._____

8. The proper method of laying up a steam boiler, for a period of less than one month, is to
    A. drain all the water and let the boiler dry out
    B. fill it with treated water to the top of the tubes
    C. fill it with treated water to the stop valve
    D. fill it with treated water to the level of the upper try cock

9. In the winter time, heating complaints by tenants should be investigated
    A. only if there are several complaints from one building
    B. only if the outside temperature is below 40°F
    C. immediately
    D. by the assistant superintendent

10. Compared to the input of an electric ignition transformer associated with #6 oil burners, the output is _____ voltage, _____ current.
    A. higher; higher
    B. higher; lower
    C. lower; higher
    D. lower; lower

11. A pressure regulator valve in a compressed air line should be
    A. preceded by a water and oil separator
    B. preceded by a solenoid valve
    C. followed by a water and oil separator
    D. followed by a solenoid valve

12. A preventive maintenance program in a boiler room should provide for the routine periodic replacement of
    A. badly leaking boiler tubes
    B. electric motors
    C. safety valve springs
    D. programmer electronic tubes

13. Steam-heated hot water tank coils can be tested for leaks by
    A. chemically testing the domestic hot water leaving the tank
    B. chemically testing the condensate leaving the coil
    C. pressure testing the domestic water in the tank
    D. pressure testing the condensate return

14. The chemical which is added to boiler water to reduce its oxygen content is sodium
    A. carbonate
    B. chloride
    C. alginate
    D. sulphite

15. Wear in the sleeve bearings of an electric motor is MOST likely to result in a change in the
    A. pole spacing
    B. armature balance
    C. air gap
    D. line frequency

16. *Found reading* and *left reading* are terms associated with 16.____
    A. petrometers
    B. electric meters
    C. gas meters
    D. water meters

17. The FIRST priority in snow removal in a housing project is to remove 17.____
    snow from the
    A. building entrance steps and entrance landings
    B. perimeter sidewalks
    C. access to fuel oil fill lines and fire hydrants
    D. interior sidewalks leading from buildings to perimeter sidewalks

18. On Memorial Day, the National Flag should be flown at 18.____
    A. full staff all day
    B. half staff in the morning and full staff from noon to sunset
    C. half staff all day
    D. full staff in the morning and at half staff from noon to sunset

19. The common name for a tree called Quercus Alba is 19.____
    A. pine
    B. maple
    C. oak
    D. cedar

20. A tree which is considered to be suitable for street curb planting should 20.____
    A. grow rapidly
    B. have colorful foliage
    C. be an evergreen
    D. be straight and symmetrical

21. A roofing bond is 21.____
    A. the material used to cement the roofing layers to each other
    B. a guarantee by the manufacturer of the roofing material
    C. a guarantee by the contractor who installed the roof
    D. a vapor barrier

22. Window shade cloth has a calculated service life of _____ years. 22.____
    A. 2   B. 4   C. 6   D. 8

23. A resin-base floor finish USUALLY 23.____
    A. gives the highest luster of all floor finishes
    B. cannot be used on asphalt tile
    C. must be applied in heavy coats
    D. provides an anti-slip surface

24. The cause of paint blisters on wood is USUALLY 24.____
    A. moisture under the paint coat
    B. too thick a coat of paint
    C. too much oil in the paint
    D. plaster pores not sealed properly

25. When waxing asphalt tile floors, the wax should be applied in several thin coats because
    A. one thick coat takes longer to apply
    B. it will dry faster and harder
    C. it is a more economical method
    D. the pores of the tile will be able to absorb the wax more readily

    25._____

26. A supplier quotes a list price of $14.00 for a replacement part less discounts of 25, 10 and 5 percent. The cost of the item is MOST NEARLY
    A. $5.50   B. $6.00   C. $8.50   D. $9.00

    26._____

27. Assuming that it requires 6 man-days to replace a sidewalk 4 feet wide x 120 feet long, then a similar sidewalk 8 feet wide x 78 feet long would require MOST NEARLY _____ man-days.
    A. 6   B. 8   C. 10   D. 14

    27._____

28. The initials S.S., as used in connection with window glass, means
    A. single strength
    B. single silicon
    C. sharp section
    D. striated surface

    28._____

29. If a screwed galvanized iron fitting is used in a copper or brass line, the MOST probable result would be that the
    A. galvanized iron fitting will rust quickly
    B. brass line will have to be replaced
    C. galvanized fitting will outlast the brass line
    D. brass line will corrode

    29._____

30. A plumbing sketch is drawn to a scale of 1/8" = 1 foot. A horizontal water line measuring 6 3/4" on the sketch would be equivalent to _____ feet of water pipe.
    A. 27   B. 41   C. 54   D. 64

    30._____

31. The tool that holds the die when threading a 2" pipe is called a
    A. yoke
    B. punch
    C. vise
    D. stock

    31._____

32. Of the following, the BEST fastener to use in a hollow wall is the _____ bolt.
    A. expansion
    B. carriage
    C. machine nut and
    D. toggle

    32._____

33. A 5 hp, 3 phase, 208-volt squirrel cage motor is USUALLY started by means of a(n)
    A. compensator
    B. across the line starter
    C. reduced voltage starter
    D. 3 point starting box

34. When using a voltmeter in testing an electric circuit, the voltmeter should be connected
    A. across the circuit
    B. in series with the circuit
    C. in parallel or series with the circuit
    D. in series with the active element

35. The coloring material in an exterior wall paint is called the
    A. solvent
    B. lacquer
    C. vehicle
    D. pigment

KEY (CORRECT ANSWERS)

1. C	11. A	21. B	31. D
2. A	12. D	22. C	32. D
3. D	13. B	23. D	33. B
4. A	14. D	24. A	34. A
5. D	15. C	25. B	35. D
6. A	16. B	26. D	
7. B	17. C	27. B	
8. C	18. B	28. A	
9. C	19. C	29. A	
10. B	20. D	30. C	

TEST 2

DIRECTIONS: Each question or incomplete statement is followed by several suggested answers or completions. Select the one that BEST answers the question or completes the statement. *PRINT THE LETTER OF THE CORRECT ANSWER IN THE SPACE AT THE RIGHT.*

1. The refrigerant MOST often used in household refrigerators is
    A. argon
    B. lithium bromide
    C. ammonia
    D. freon-12

    1._____

2. When tie or identical low bids are submitted for a competitive contract under $1,000 by two bidders, the successful bidder may be selected by
    A. requesting a new bid from a third party
    B. tossing a coin
    C. drawing lots
    D. requesting new bids from all the bidders and selecting the lowest bid

    2._____

3. The one of the following which is LEAST important in developing a budget for the next fiscal year for project maintenance is the
    A. adequacy of the current year's budget
    B. changes in workload that can be anticipated
    C. budget restrictions indicated in a memorandum covering budget preparations
    D. staff reassignments which are expected during the next fiscal year

    3._____

4. The LEAST likely subject to be discussed at a planning meeting with assistant superintendents and foremen is the
    A. allocation of responsibility for the phases of administration
    B. provision for coordination and follow-up
    C. setting goals for each supervisor's section
    D. assignment of tasks to individual workers

    4._____

5. From the standpoint of equal opportunity, the MOST critical item that a superintendent should focus on is
    A. assigning only minority workers to supervisory positions
    B. helping minority employees to upgrade their knowledge so they may qualify for higher positions
    C. placing minority workers in job categories above their present level of ability so that they can "sink" or "swim"
    D. disregarding merit system principles

    5._____

6. After careful deliberation, you have decided that one of your workers should be disciplined. It is MOST important that the
    A. discipline be severe for best results
    B. discipline be delayed as long as possible
    C. worker understands why he is being disciplined
    D. other workers be consulted before the discipline is administered

    6._____

7. Of the following, the MOST important qualities of an employee chosen for a supervisory position are
    A. education and intelligence
    B. interest in the objectives and activities of the agency
    C. skill in performing the type of work to be supervised
    D. knowledge of the work and leadership ability

8. A tenant complains to you that he was wet by the spray from a garden hose handled carelessly by one of your workers and that he can identify the worker. The BEST course of action is for you to
    A. express regret and assure the tenant that you will caution the worker
    B. try to convince the tenant that he did not get too wet
    C. assure the tenant that charges will be preferred against the worker
    D. arrange a meeting between tenant and worker and make the worker apologize

9. In preparing a report to his supervisor, a superintendent should
    A. include irrelevant matters to show a greater grasp of the problem
    B. not allow anyone to read and criticize the draft of the report for fear that he will seem incompetent
    C. prepare an outline before writing the draft of the report
    D. always question whether or not the report is necessary

10. A superintendent who is preparing a report on a study which was requested by his supervisor should make the FIRST section of the report a discussion of the
    A. situation which exists currently
    B. method of instituting the recommendations
    C. objections to the report
    D. additional equipment needed to carry out the recommendations

11. A superintendent should read the work orders for the maintenance men each morning so that
    A. every work order is completed the day it is received
    B. all work orders are handled in chronological order regardless of the kind of work involved
    C. the work which the maintenance men do not like to do is not postponed continually
    D. the maintenance men know that you are checking up on them every minute of the day

12. MOST tenants in a housing project will
    A. separate in their minds the actions of a superintendent and the policies of the housing authority
    B. consider what the superintendent does as the policy of the housing authority
    C. realize that superintendents will follow policies that are undesirable to the housing authority
    D. make allowances for the policies a superintendent follows

13. Mortar joints in old brickwork are BEST repaired by
    A. setting
    B. framing
    C. taping
    D. pointing

14. An equipment rental allowance includes the rental charge plus 9%. If a piece of equipment is rented for 11 days at $36 per day, the total equipment allowance is MOST NEARLY
    A. $360   B. $390   C. $420   D. $450

15. The extinguishing agent in a soda-acid fire extinguisher is
    A. water
    B. hydrochloric acid
    C. sodium bicarbonate
    D. carbon dioxide

16. A building heated by an oil-fired boiler used 3,500 gallons of oil during a period of 2100 degree days. The number of gallons of oil that probably would be burned by the same building over a period of 1800 degree days is
    A. 2700   B. 3000   C. 3400   D. 3700

17. Of the following, the BEST chemical to use to melt ice on pavements is
    A. carbon tetrachloride
    B. calcium chloride
    C. potassium hydroxide
    D. sodium fluoride

18. The MAIN purpose of periodic inspection and tests of electrical equipment is to
    A. encourage workers to take better care of the equipment
    B. familiarize the workers with the equipment
    C. keep the workers busy during otherwise slack periods
    D. discover minor faults before they develop into major faults

19. The greatest benefit of job evaluation is in
    A. placing the blame for inefficiency
    B. testing the intelligence of custodial workers
    C. eliminating duplication of activities
    D. determining efficiency ratings

20. The current rating of the fuse to use in a lighting circuit is determined by the
    A. connected load
    B. line voltage
    C. capacity of the wiring
    D. rating of the switch

21. Portable fire extinguishers which are suitable for Class C fires should be identified by the letter C inside a
    A. triangle
    B. circle
    C. square
    D. five-point star

    21._____

22. In the piping system for domestic gas supply,
    A. risers must have a drip leg and cap at the bottom
    B. gasketed unions are used to join pipes
    C. couplings with running threads are used to join pipes
    D. composition disc globe valves are used to throttle the gas

    22._____

23. A cast iron soil pipe-bend having an angle of 45 degrees is COMMONLY called a _____ bend.
    A. 1/16 B. 1/8 C. 1/4 D. return

    23._____

24. Of the following, the LEAST likely cause of faulty atomization of fuel oil in a rotary cup oil burner is
    A. too low an oil temperature
    B. too low an oil pressure
    C. insufficient secondary air
    D. insufficient primary air

    24._____

25. In order to minimize the labor involved in replacing an electric motor, which is directly connected to a centrifugal house pump, the specification for the new motor should include the
    A. shaft size
    B. NEMA frame size
    C. end bell size
    D. NEMA design letter

    25._____

26. The supervisor of a large group of maintenance workers will most likely find that the GREATEST number of them will be motivated by
    A. letting them plan and control their own work
    B. giving them more responsibility
    C. supervising them very closely
    D. considering each of them individually and treating them accordingly

    26._____

27. An example of a non-flammable liquid is
    A. floor sealer
    B. kerosene
    C. carbon tetrachloride
    D. benzene

    27._____

28. Which of the following malfunctions is MOST hazardous to life? 28._____
    A. Short circuit in an outlet box
    B. Gas leak from a stove connection
    C. Water leak behind a kitchen sink
    D. Steam leak from a stop valve

29. A supervisor observes that there is a constant backlog of work tickets, 29._____
    which results in a long delay between the time when a complaint is
    reported by a tenant and when the work is completed.
    In handling this situation, the supervisor should
    A. ignore the situation if he is certain he can avoid being blamed for it
    B. ignore the situation because it is really the responsibility of the
       superintendent
    C. explain the situation to the superintendent and recommend waiting
       until the situation gets so bad that the central office will realize that
       more permanent maintenance men are needed
    D. explain the situation to the superintendent and recommend that he
       request the loan of several maintenance men from the central
       office for sufficient time to reduce the backlog to normal

30. A supervisor assigns a maintenance man to do an emergency job and 30._____
    gives him the authority to obtain the help and equipment he needs to
    complete the job.
    Under these circumstances, FINAL responsibility for the job
    A. belongs to the maintenance man
    B. remains with the supervisor
    C. cannot be determined
    D. is shared between the maintenance man and the supervisor

KEY (CORRECT ANSWERS)

1. D	11. C	21. B
2. C	12. B	22. A
3. D	13. D	23. B
4. D	14. C	24. C
5. B	15. A	25. B
6. C	16. B	26. D
7. D	17. B	27. C
8. A	18. D	28. B
9. C	19. C	29. D
10. A	20. C	30. B

EXAMINATION SECTION
TEST 1

DIRECTIONS: Each question or incomplete statement is followed by several suggested answers or completions. Select the one that BEST answers the question or completes the statement. *PRINT THE LETTER OF THE CORRECT ANSWER IN THE SPACE AT THE RIGHT.*

1. Before starting any lawn mowing, the distance between the blade and a flat surface should be measured with a ruler.
   The distance should be such that the cut of the grass above the ground is _____ inch(es).
   A. 1 B. 1½ C. 2 D. 3

   1._____

2. Strainers in a number 6 fuel oil system should be checked once a
   A. day B. week C. month D. year

   2._____

3. The spinning cup on a rotary cup oil burner should be cleaned
   A. once a day
   B. once a week
   C. every 2 weeks
   D. once a month

   3._____

4. Terrazzo floors should be cleaned daily with a
   A. damp mop using clear water
   B. damp mop using a strong alkaline solution
   C. damp mop treated with vegetable oil

   4._____

5. New installations of vinyl-asbestos floor should
   A. never be machine scrubbed
   B. be dry buffed weekly
   C. be swept daily, using an oily compound
   D. never be swept with treated dust mops

   5._____

6. Standpipe fire hose shall be inspected
   A. monthly
   B. quarterly
   C. semi-annually
   D. annually

   6._____

7. All portable fire extinguishers shall be inspected once
   A. a year
   B. a month
   C. a week
   D. every 3 months

   7._____

8. Soda-acid and foam-type fire extinguishers shall be discharged and recharged AT LEAST once
   A. each year
   B. every 2 years
   C. every 6 months
   D. each month

   8._____

9. Elevator *safeties* under the car shall be tested once each
   A. day   B. week   C. month   D. quarter

10. Key-type fire alarms in public school buildings shall be tested
    A. daily   B. weekly   C. monthly   D. quarterly

11. Combustion efficiency can be determined from an appropriate chart used in conjunction with
    A. steam temperature and steam pressure
    B. flue gas temperature and percentage of CO_2
    C. flue gas temperature and fuel heating value
    D. oil temperature and steam pressure

12. In the combustion of common fuels, the MAJOR boiler heat loss is due to
    A. incomplete combustion   B. moisture in the fuel
    C. heat radiation   D. heat lost in the flue gases

13. The MOST important reason for blowing down a boiler water column and gauge glass is to
    A. prevent the gauge glass level from rising too high
    B. relieve stresses in the gauge glass
    C. insure a true water level reading
    D. insure a true pressure gauge reading

14. The secondary voltage of a transformer used for ignition in a fuel oil burner has a range of MOST NEARLY _____ volts to _____ volts.
    A. 120; 240   B. 440; 660   C. 660; 1,200   D. 5,000; 15,000

15. Assume that during the month of April there were 3 days with an average outdoor temperature of 30°F, 7 days with 40°F, 10 days with 50°F, 3 days with 60°F, and 7 days with 65°F.
    The number of degree days for the month was
    A. 330   B. 445   C. 595   D. 1,150

16. The pH of boiler feedwater is USUALLY maintained within the range of
    A. 4 to 5   B. 6 to 7   C. 10 to 12   D. 13 to 14

17. The admission of steam to the coils of a domestic hot water supply tank is regulated by a(n)
    A. pressure regulating valve   B. immersion type temperature gauge
    C. check valve   D. thermostatic control valve

18. The device which senses primary air failure in a rotary cup oil burner is USUALLY called a(n)
    A. vaporstate   B. anemometer
    C. venture   D. pressure gauge

3 (#1)

19. The device which starts and stops the flow of oil into an automatic rotary cup oil burner is USUALLY called a(n) _____ valve. 19.____
    A. magnetic oil   B. oil metering   C. oil check   D. relief

20. A vacuum breaker used on a steam-heated domestic hot water tank is USUALLY connected to the 20.____
    A. circulating pump   B. tank wall
    C. aquastat   D. steam coil flange

21. A vacuum pump in a low pressure steam heating system which is equipped with a float switch, a vacuum switch, a magnetic starter, and a selector switch, can be operated on 21.____
    A. float, vacuum, or automatic   B. float, vacuum, or continuous
    C. vacuum, automatic, or continuous   D. float, automatic, or continuous

22. If the temperature of the condensate returning to the vacuum pump in a low pressure steam vacuum heating system is above 180°F, the trouble may be caused by 22.____
    A. faulty radiator traps
    B. room thermostats being set too high
    C. uninsulated return lines
    D. too many radiators being shut off

23. A feedwater regulator operates to 23.____
    A. shut down the burner when the water is low
    B. maintain the water in the boiler at a predetermined level
    C. drain the water in the boiler
    D. regulate the temperature of the feedwater

24. An automatically fired steam boiler is equipped with an automatic low water cut-off.
    The low water cut-off is USUALLY actuated by 24.____
    A. steam pressure   B. fuel pressure
    C. float action   D. water temperature

25. Low pressure steam or an electric heater is USUALLY required for heating _____ fuel. 25.____
    A. #1   B. #2   C. #4   D. #6

KEY (CORRECT ANSWERS)

1.	C	11.	B
2.	A	12.	D
3.	A	13.	C
4.	A	14.	D
5.	B	15.	B
6.	B	16.	C
7.	B	17.	D
8.	A	18.	A
9.	C	19.	A
10.	A	20.	D

21. D
22. A
23. B
24. C
25. D

TEST 2

DIRECTIONS: Each question or incomplete statement is followed by several suggested answers or completions. Select the one that BEST answers the question or completes the statement. *PRINT THE LETTER OF THE CORRECT ANSWER IN THE SPACE AT THE RIGHT.*

1. A compound gauge is calibrated to read 1.____
   A. pressure only
   B. vacuum only
   C. vacuum and pressure
   D. temperature and humidity

2. In a mechanical pressure-atomizing type oil burner, the oil is automized by using an automizing tip and 2.____
   A. steam pressure
   B. pump pressure
   C. compressed air
   D. a spinning cup

3. A good over-the-fire draft in a natural draft furnace should be APPROXIMATELY _____ inch(es) of water _____. 3.____
   A. 5.0; positive pressure
   B. 0.05; positive pressure
   C. 0.05; vacuum
   D. 5.0; vacuum

4. When it is necessary to add chemicals to a heating boiler, it should be done 4.____
   A. immediately after boiler blowdown
   B. after the boiler has been cleaned internally of sludge, scale, and other foreign matter
   C. at periods when condensate flow to the boiler is small
   D. at a time when there is a heavy flow of condensate to the boiler

5. The modutrol motor on a rotary cup oil burner burning #6 fuel oil automatically operates the primary air damper, 5.____
   A. secondary air damper, and oil metering valve
   B. secondary air damper, and magnetic oil valve
   C. oil metering valve, and magnetic oil valve
   D. and magnetic oil valve

6. The manual-reset pressuretrol is classified as a _____ Control. 6.____
   A. Safety and Operating
   B. Limit and Operating
   C. Limit and Safety
   D. Limit, Operating, and Safety

7. Sodium sulphite is added to boiler feedwater to 7.____
   A. avoid caustic embrittlement
   B. increase the pH value
   C. reduce the tendency of foaming in the steam drum
   D. remove dissolved oxygen

8. Neat cement is a mixture of cement, 8.____
   A. putty, and water
   B. and water
   C. lime, and water
   D. salt, and water

9. In a concrete mix of 1:2:4, the 2 refers to the amount of 9.____
   A. sand B. cement C. stone D. water

10. The word *natatorium* means MOST NEARLY a(n) 10.____
    A. auditorium B. playroom
    C. gymnasium D. indoor swimming pool

11. Plated metal surfaces which are protected by a thin coat of clear lacquer should be cleaned with a(n) 11.____
    A. abrasive compound B. liquid polish
    C. mild soap solution D. lemon oil solution

12. Wet mop filler replacements are ordered by 12.____
    A. length B. weight
    C. number of strands D. trade number

13. The BEST way to determine the value of a cleaning material is by 13.____
    A. performance testing
    B. manufacturer's literature
    C. written specifications
    D. interviews with manufacturer's salesman

14. Instructions on a container of cleaning compound state: *Mix one pound of compound in 5 gallons of water.* 14.____
    Using these instructions, the amount of compound which should be added to 15 quarts of water is MOST NEARLY _____ ounces.
    A. 3 B. 8 C. 12 D. 48

15. The MOST usual cause of paint blisters is 15.____
    A. too much oil in the paint B. moisture under the paint coat
    C. a heavy coat of paint D. improper drying of paint

16. The floor that should NOT be machine scrubbed is a(n) 16.____
    A. lobby B. lunchroom
    C. gymnasium D. auditorium aisle

17. Pick-up sweeping in a public building is the occasional removal of the more conspicuous loose dirt from corridors and lobbies. 17.____
    This type of sweeping should be done
    A. after scrubbing or waving of floors
    B. with the aid of a sweeping compound
    C. at night after school hours
    D. during regular school hours

18. According to recommended practice, when a steam boiler is taken out of service for a long period of time, the boiler drum should FIRST be
    A. drained completely while the water is hot (above 212°F)
    B. drained completely after the water has been cooled down to 180°F
    C. filled completely without draining
    D. filled to the level of the top try cock

19. The prevention and control of vermin and rodents in a building is PRIMARILY a matter of
    A. maintaining good housekeeping on a continuous basis
    B. periodic use of an exterminator's service
    C. calling in the exterminator when necessary
    D. cleaning the building thoroughly during school vacation

20. If it is not possible to plant new shrubs immediately upon delivery in the spring, they should be stored in a(n)
    A. sheltered outdoor area
    B. unsheltered outdoor area
    C. boiler room
    D. warm place indoors

21. Peat moss is generally used for its
    A. food value
    B. nitrogen
    C. alkalinity
    D. moisture retaining quality

22. The legal minimum age of employees engaged for cleaning windows in the state is _____ years.
    A. 16   B. 17   C. 18   D. 21

23. The MAIN classification of lumber used for construction purposes is known as _____ lumber.
    A. industrial   B. commercial   C. finish   D. yard

24. Specifications concerning window cleaners' anchors and safety belts must be in compliance with the rules and regulations outlined in the
    A. state labor law and board of standards and appeals
    B. city building code
    C. fire department safety manual
    D. national protection code

25. Pruning of street trees is the responsibility of the
    A. custodian-engineer
    B. board of education
    C. department of parks
    D. borough president's office

KEY (CORRECT ANSWERS)

1.	C	11.	C
2.	B	12.	B
3.	C	13.	A
4.	D	14.	C
5.	A	15.	B
6.	C	16.	C
7.	D	17.	D
8.	B	18.	B
9.	A	19.	A
10.	D	20.	A

21.	D
22.	C
23.	D
24.	A
25.	C

EXAMINATION SECTION
TEST 1

DIRECTIONS: Each question or incomplete statement is followed by several suggested answers or completions. Select the one that BEST answers the question or completes the statement. *PRINT THE LETTER OF THE CORRECT ANSWER IN THE SPACE AT THE RIGHT.*

1. Oil soaked waste and rags *should be* 1.____

    A. deposited in a self-closing metal can
    B. piled in the open
    C. stored in the supply closet
    D. rolled up and be available for the next job

2. Inspection for safety should be included as part of the custodian-engineer's _____ inspection. 2.____

    A. daily   B. weekly
    C. monthly   D. quarterly

3. Of the following classifications, the one which pertains to fires in electrical equipment is Class _____. 3.____

    A. A   B. B   C. C   D. D

4. The type of portable fire extinguisher which is *particularly* suited for extinguishing flammable liquid fires is the _____ type. 4.____

    A. soda-acid   B. foam
    C. pump tank   D. loaded stream

5. Of the following liquids, the one which has the LOWEST flash point is 5.____

    A. kerosene   B. gasoline
    C. benzene   D. carbon tetrachloride

6. When giving first aid to an injured person, which *one* of the following should you NOT do? 6.____

    A. Administer medication internally
    B. Send for a physician
    C. Control bleeding
    D. Treat for shock

7. In reference to fire fighting, fires are of such complexity that 7.____

    A. no plans or methods of attack can be formulated in advance
    B. the problem must be considered in advance and methods of attack formulated
    C. an appointed committee is necessary to direct fighting at the fire
    D. no planned procedures can be relied on

8. The heat of a soldering copper should be tested 8.____

    A. with solder
    B. by holding it near kraft paper

19

C. by holding it near your hand
D. with water

9. Safety on the job is BEST assured by

   A. keeping alert
   B. following every rule
   C. working very slowly
   D. never working alone

10. One important use of accident reports is to provide information that may be used to reduce the possibility of similar accidents.
    The MOST valuable entry on the report for this purpose is the

    A. time lost due to accident
    B. date of the occurrence
    C. injury sustained by victim
    D. cause of the accident

11. Suppose that you are the custodian-engineer and an employee works for you at the rate of $8.70 per hour with time and one-half paid for time worked after 40 hours in one week. His gross pay for working 53 hours in one week is, *most nearly,*

    A. $461.10   B. $482.10   C. $487.65   D. $517.65

12. Suppose that you are the custodian-engineer and one of your employees has gotten gross earnings of $437.10 for the week, all of which is subject to Social Security deductions at the rate of 7.05%.
    The amount which should be deducted from the employee's gross earnings for the week is, *most nearly,*

    A. $21.70   B. $28.40   C. $29.32   D. $30.82

13. The MINIMUM number of gate valves usually required in a by-pass around a steam trap is

    A. 1   B. 2   C. 3   D. 4

14. A 2-inch standard steel pipe, as compared with a 2-inch extra-heavy steel pipe, has the *same*

    A. wall thickness
    B. inside diameter
    C. outside diameter
    D. weight per linear foot

15. A short piece of pipe with a standard male pipe thread on one end and a locknut thread on the other end is *usually* called a(n)

    A. close nipple
    B. tank nipple
    C. coupling
    D. union

16. Dies are used by plumbers to

    A. ream out the inside of pipes
    B. thread pipes
    C. bevel the ends of pipes
    D. make-up solder joints

17. Of the following types of pipe, the one which is MOST brittle is 17.____

    A. brass   B. copper
    C. cast iron   D. wrought iron

18. The PRIMARY function of a trap in a drainage system is to 18.____

    A. prevent gases from flowing into the building
    B. produce an efficient flushing action
    C. prevent articles accidentally dropped into the drainage system from entering the sewer
    D. prevent the water backing up

19. If a plumbing fixture is allowed to stand unused for a long time, its trap is apt to lose its seal by 19.____

    A. evaporation   B. capillary action
    C. siphonage   D. condensation

20. The pipe fitting used to connect a 1¼" pipe directly to a 1" pipe in a straight line is called a(n) 20.____

    A. union   B. nipple   C. elbow   D. reducer

21. The BEST procedure to follow when replacing a blown fuse is to 21.____

    A. immediately replace it with the same size fuse
    B. immediately replace it with a larger size fuse
    C. immediately replace it with a smaller size fuse
    D. correct the cause of the fuse failure and replace it with the correct size

22. The amperage rating of the fuse to be used in an electrical circuit is determined by the 22.____

    A. size of the connected load
    B. size of the wire in the circuit
    C. voltage of the circuit
    D. ambient temperature

23. In a 208-volt, 3-phase, 4-wire circuit, the voltage, in volts, from any line to the grounded neutral is, *approximately,* 23.____

    A. 208   B. 150   C. 120   D. zero

24. The device *commonly* used to change an A.C. voltage to a D.C. voltage is called a 24.____

    A. transformer   B. rectifier
    C. relay   D. capacitor or condenser

25. Where conduit enters a knock-out in an outlet box, it should be provided with a 25.____

    A. bushing on the inside and outside with a locknut
    B. locknut on the inside and bushing on the outside
    C. union on the outside and a nipple on the inside
    D. nipple on the outside and a union on the inside

KEY (CORRECT ANSWERS)

1.	A	11.	D
2.	A	12.	D
3.	C	13.	C
4.	B	14.	C
5.	B	15.	B
6.	A	16.	B
7.	B	17.	C
8.	A	18.	A
9.	A	19.	A
10.	D	20.	D

21. D
22. B
23. C
24. B
25. A

TEST 2

DIRECTIONS: Each question or incomplete statement is followed by several suggested answers or completions. Select the one that BEST answers the question or completes the Statement. *PRINT THE LETTER OF THE CORRECT ANSWER IN THE SPACE AT THE RIGHT.*

1. The electric circuit to a ten kilowatt electric hot water heater which is automatically controlled by an aquastat will *also* require a   1.____

   A. transistor
   B. choke coil
   C. magnetic contactor
   D. limit switch

2. An electric power consumption meter usually indicates the power used in   2.____

   A. watts
   B. volt-hours
   C. amperes
   D. kilowatt-hours

3. Of the following sizes of copper wire, the one which can *safely* carry the GREATEST amount of amperes is   3.____

   A. 14 ga. stranded
   B. 12 ga. stranded
   C. 12 ga. solid
   D. 10 ga. solid

4. A flexible coupling is PRIMARILY used to   4.____

   A. allow for imperfect alignment of two joining shafts
   B. allow for slight differences in shaft diameters
   C. insure perfect alignment of the joining shafts
   D. reduce fast starting of the machinery

5. The one of the following statements concerning lubricating oil which is CORRECT is: 5.____

   A. SAE 10 is heavier and more viscous than SAE 30.
   B. Diluting lubricating oil with gasoline increases its viscosity
   C. Oil reduces friction between moving parts
   D. In hot weather, thin oil is preferable to heavy oil

6. The MAIN purpose of periodic inspections and tests made on mechanical equipment is to   6.____

   A. make the operating men familiar with the equipment
   B. keep the maintenance men busy during otherwise slack periods
   C. discover minor faults before they develop into serious breakdowns
   D. encourage the men to take better care of the equipment

7. The one of the following bearing types which is NOT classified as a roller bearing is   7.____

   A. radial   B. angular   C. thrust   D. babbitt

8. In a wire rope, when a number of wires are laid left-handed into a strand and the strand laid right-handed around a hemp rope center, the wire rope is *commonly* known as a   8.____

   A. right-lay, Lang-lay rope
   B. left-lay, Lang-lay rope
   C. left-lay, regular-lay rope
   D. right-lay, regular-lay rope

23

9. The chemical which is NOT used for disinfecting swimming pools is 9.___

   A. ammonia
   B. calcium hypochloride
   C. chlorine
   D. liquified chlorine

10. The one of the following V-belt sections which has the HIGHEST horsepower-belt rating is _____ section 10.___

   A. A
   B. B
   C. C
   D. D

11. An air compressor which is driven by an electric motor is *usually* started and stopped automatically by a(n) 11.___

   A. unloader
   B. pressure regulator valve
   C. float switch
   D. pressure switch

12. The volume in cubic feet of a cylindrical tank, 6 ft. in diameter by 35 ft. long, is, *most nearly*, 12.___

   A. 210
   B. 990
   C. 1,260
   D. 3,960

13. If the directions given by your superior are NOT clear, the BEST thing for you to do is to 13.___

   A. ask to have the directions repeated and clarified
   B. proceed to do the work taking a chance on doing the right thing
   C. do nothing until some later time when you can find out exactly what is wanted
   D. ask one of the other men in your crew what he would do under the circumstances

14. Of the following procedures concerning grievances of subordinate personnel, the custodian-engineer should maintain an attitude of 14.___

   A. paying little attention to little grievances
   B. being very alert to grievances and make adjustments in existing conditions to appease all personnel
   C. knowing the most frequent causes of grievances and strive to prevent them from arising
   D. maintain rigid discipline of a nature that smoothes out all grievances

15. Of the following, the BEST course of action to take to settle a dispute or conflict between two employees is to 15.___

   A. insist that the two employees settle the case between themselves
   B. call in each one separately and, after hearing their cases presented, decide the issue
   C. bring both in for a conference at the same time and make the decision in their presence
   D. have both present their points of view and arguments in written memoranda and, on this basis, make your decision

16. If, as a custodian-engineer, you discover an error in your report submitted to the main office, you should 16.___

   A. do nothing, since it is possible that one error will have little effect on the total report
   B. wait until the error is discovered in the main office and then offer to work overtime to correct it
   C. go directly to the supervisor in the main office after working hours and ask him unofficially to correct the error
   D. notify the main office immediately so that the error can be corrected, if necessary

17. There are a considerable number of forms and reports to be submitted on schedule by the custodian-engineer. The *advisable* method of accomplishing this duty is to

    A. fill out the reports at off times during the days when you have free time
    B. schedule a definite period to the work week for completing these forms and reports
    C. assign your foremen or cleaner to handle all these forms for you and to have them available on time
    D. classify or group the forms and reports and fill out only one of each group and refer the other forms or reports to the ones completed

18. A custodian-engineer can BEST evaluate the quality of work performed by custodial personnel by

    A. periodic inspection of the building's cleanliness
    B. studying the time records or personnel
    C. reviewing the building cleaning expenditures
    D. analyzing complaints of building occupants

19. Assume that you are the custodian-engineer and one of your employees wants to talk with you about a grievance. Of the following actions, the LEAST desirable action for you to take is to

    A. listen sympathetically
    B. conduct the discussion openly in the presence of the workforce
    C. try to get his point of view
    D. endeavor to obtain all the facts

20. Of the following factors, the one which is LEAST important in evaluating an employee and his work is his

    A. dependability   B. quantity of work
    C. quality of work   D. education and training

21. Supervision of a group of people engaged in building cleaning operations should NOT include supervision of

    A. time spent in cleaning operations
    B. utilization of official rest and lunch periods
    C. cleaning methods
    D. materials used for various cleaning jobs

22. Of the following methods, the BEST one to utilize in assigning custodial personnel to clean a multi-floor public building, is to

    A. allow the cleaners to pick their rooms or area assignment out of a hat
    B. have the supervisor make specific room or area assignments to each cleaner separately
    C. rotate room and area assignments daily according to a chart posted on the bulletin board
    D. let a different member of the group make the room or area assignments each week

23. Assume that you are the custodian-engineer and that you have discovered a bottle of liquor in one of your employees' locker.
The BEST course of action to take is to

    A. fire him immediately
    B. explain to him that liquor should not be brought into a school building and that a repetition may result in disciplinary action
    C. suspend him until the end of the week and take him back only on a probational basis
    D. assemble the staff and tell them they are all equally guilty for not having reported the matter to you

24. Of the following items, the one which is the LEAST important in the preparation of a report is that the report

    A. is brief, but to the point
    B. uses the prescribed form if there is one
    C. contains extra copies
    D. is accurate

25. In order to have building employees willing to follow standardized cleaning and maintenance procedures, the supervisor must *be prepared to*

    A. work alongside the employees
    B. demonstrate the reasonableness of the procedures
    C. offer incentive pay for their utilization
    D. allow the employees the free use of the time saved by their adoption

KEY (CORRECT ANSWERS)

1.	C	11.	D
2.	D	12.	B
3.	D	13.	A
4.	A	14.	C
5.	C	15.	C
6.	C	16.	D
7.	D	17.	B
8.	D	18.	A
9.	A	19.	B
10.	D	20.	D

21. B
22. B
23. B
24. C
25. B

EXAMINATION SECTION
TEST 1

DIRECTIONS: Each question or incomplete statement is followed by several suggested answers or completions. Select the one that BEST answers the question or completes the statement. *PRINT THE LETTER OF THE CORRECT ANSWER IN THE SPACE AT THE RIGHT.*

1. Of the following, the one action which will MOST likely prolong the useful life of a hair broom is to

    A. store it after use by hanging it by the handle
    B. keep the bristles moist at all times
    C. use the wooden back of the broom to hammer down any nails which protrude from the floor surface
    D. lean heavily on the broom when sweeping so that all the dirt is moved with one stroke

    1._____

2. Sweep cloths are often chemically treated with

    A. water   B. scouring powder
    C. cornstarch   D. mineral oil

    2._____

3. In the event of a temporary shortage of custodial help at a school, FIRST priority should be given to cleaning the _____ office.

    A. dean's   B. general
    C. medical   D. superintendent's

    3._____

4. The one of the following which should be used to remove chewing gum from an asphalt tile floor is

    A. coarse sandpaper   B. a putty knife
    C. lemon oil   D. gasoline

    4._____

5. The BEST cleaning tool to use to dust the tops of radiator covers is a

    A. wet sponge   B. bowl brush
    C. counter brush D. corn broom

    5._____

6. The BEST cleaning tool to use to clean a slate blackboard is a

    A. wet sponge   B. bowl brush
    C. counter brush D. corn broom

    6._____

7. The BEST cleaning tool to use to clean a commode is a

    A. wet sponge   B. bowl brush
    C. counter brush D. corn broom

    7._____

8. The BEST cleaning tool to use to sweep a rough concrete floor is a

    A. wet sponge   B. bowl brush
    C. counter brush D. corn broom

    8._____

9. For wet mopping the floor of a corridor by hand, the MINIMUM number of pails needed is

    A. one   B. two   C. three   D. four

    9._____

10. A comparison of wet mopping by hand with scrubbing by hand indicates that mopping

   A. needs more cleaning solution
   B. is more time consuming
   C. requires twice as much water
   D. is less effective on hardened soil

11. Of the following, the MOST important consideration when choosing a cleaning agent for use in a building is the

   A. high cost of cleaning agents when compared to labor costs
   B. effect it has on the amount of labor required
   C. kind of odor it gives off
   D. quantity on hand

12. Of the following, the BEST way that a custodial foreman can reduce waste in the use of cleaning supplies is to

   A. dole out the supplies at the beginning of the shift and collect the remainder at the end of the shift
   B. issue a storeroom key to each cleaner so that supplies can be obtained anytime
   C. train the cleaners to use the supplies and equipment properly
   D. have cleaners sign a receipt for all supplies issued

13. A detergent manufacturer recommends mixing 8 ounces of detergent in one gallon of water to prepare a cleaning solution.
    The amount of the same detergent which should be mixed with thirty gallons of water to obtain the same strength cleaning solution is _____ ounces.

   A. 24   B. 30   C. 240   D. 380

14. The floor area of a corridor 8 feet wide and 72 feet long is most nearly _____ square feet.

   A. 80   B. 420   C. 580   D. 870

15. The one of the following types of flooring which does NOT require waxing to preserve its finish is

   A. rubber tile   B. cork tile
   C. linoleum   D. terrazzo

16. The one of the following cleaning tasks which must be done MOST frequently is to

   A. damp mop the floor   B. empty the waste baskets
   C. dust the Venetian blinds   D. simonize the furniture

17. The TOTAL area of the following rooms is most nearly _____ square feet.

Room 201	1,196
Room 202	1,196
Room 203	827
Room 204	827

   A. 3,000   B. 4,000   C. 5,000   D. 6,000

18. The average area of the rooms listed in the preceding question is _____ of the total.   18._____

    A. 1/4 B. 1/3 C. 1/2 D. 3/4

19. The one of the following terms which BEST describes the size of a floor mop is   19._____

    A. 10 quart B. 32 ounce
    C. 24 inch O.D. D. 10 square feet

20. The one of the following terms which BEST describes the size of a water pail is   20._____

    A. 10 quart B. 32 ounce
    C. 24 inch O.D. D. 10 square feet

21. The one of the following terms which BEST describes the size of a floor-scrubber brush is   21._____

    A. 10 quart B. 32 ounce
    C. 24 inch O.D. D. 10 square foot

22. Of the following items, the one which is BEST to use when dusting a mahogany table is a   22._____

    A. feather duster B. treated cotton cloth
    C. crocus cloth D. wet sponge

23. The one of the following tasks which should be a *two-man* assignment is   23._____

    A. vacuum cleaning a rug
    B. sweeping a classroom
    C. washing blackboards in a classroom
    D. washing fluorescent light fixtures

24. The grease filters in a kitchen range exhaust system are usually found   24._____

    A. in the hood
    B. after the first bend in the duct
    C. on the roof
    D. in the base of the range

25. The GREATEST benefit which can result from a custodial foreman's daily inspection program occurs when the inspections are used to indicate to the employees   25._____

    A. how they can improve the work they are doing
    B. that they are being watched
    C. that the foreman is worried about losing his job
    D. that becoming a foreman will release them from manual labor

26. Of the following, the one which takes up MORE of a custodial foreman's time than any of the others is   26._____

    A. work planning and job analysis
    B. personnel problems
    C. safety and training
    D. supervision and inspection

27. Neatsfoot oil is usually used on

    A. sore feet
    B. asphalt tile floors
    C. wood furniture
    D. leather

28. Of the following tasks which are usually performed each day, when a full staff of cleaners is present, which one should the custodial foreman select to have done *only twice a week,* if his staff was temporarily reduced by one-half?

    A. Toilet cleaning
    B. Sweeping corridors
    C. Trash collection
    D. Elevator cleaning

29. The one of the following which can be used BOTH as a disinfectant and as a bleach is

    A. chlorine solution
    B. powdered whiting
    C. pine oil
    D. boric acid

30. The word *abrasive* means most nearly the same as

    A. smooth
    B. powdered
    C. scratchy
    D. sticky

31. The word *vandalism* means most nearly the same as

    A. destruction
    B. security
    C. safety
    D. juvenile

32. The one of the following which is NOT considered to be a hard floor is

    A. concrete
    B. marble
    C. terrazzo
    D. asphalt tile

33. A custodial foreman, in charge of an adequately staffed building, observes that the standard of cleanliness in the building is very poor.
    Of the following, the BEST thing he can do to raise the standard is to

    A. start a training program for the cleaners
    B. fire half of the cleaners and hire new ones
    C. reprimand the cleaner who is doing the best job, in the presence of the other cleaners
    D. clean the lobby himself so that visitors will believe the whole building is clean

34. A supervisor's FIRST step toward correcting the problem of a worker who is often late for work should be to

    A. check to see whether the worker completes his assigned work
    B. report him to higher authority
    C. talk to him to find out why he is late
    D. ignore the problem

35. One of the BEST ways for a supervisor to gain the cooperation of his employees is to

    A. encourage employees to make suggestions
    B. favor certain employees
    C. avoid complimenting good work performance
    D. find fault with everything they do

36. A night cleaner reports to the custodial foreman that he has accidentally damaged a piece of office equipment while cleaning an office.
The custodial foreman should

    A. tell him to stop cleaning the office and leave things where he found them so that no one will know he was in the office
    B. explain what happened to the occupant of the office and arrange to have the damage repaired or the equipment replaced, if possible
    C. tell the cleaner to finish cleaning the office and to deny any knowledge of the damage if anyone asks
    D. tell the cleaner he will have to pay for the damage with his own money

37. When it is necessary for a supervisor to reprimand an employee, he should do so

    A. in private
    B. only in writing
    C. in the presence of all the employees
    D. by first apologizing for the reprimand

38. When no one in a group of subordinates has ever made any complaints or ever reported having difficulty in carrying out assignments, the supervisor should realize that

    A. the group has no interest in the work
    B. his performance as a supervisor is perfect
    C. he may be making it too difficult for them to make a complaint
    D. their work is too easy

39. The one of the following for which a custodial foreman is NOT responsible is

    A. cleaning methods
    B. cleaning equipment utilization
    C. lunch time activity
    D. women's lavatory supplies

40. Of the following, the BEST way for a custodial foreman to keep his subordinates informed of new rules and regulations is to

    A. ask the union to take care of it
    B. post them on the bulletin board
    C. wait until a subordinate breaks a rule and then reprimand all of them
    D. hold meetings once a year to explain the rules

KEY (CORRECT ANSWERS)

1.	A	11.	B	21.	C	31.	A
2.	D	12.	C	22.	B	32.	D
3.	C	13.	C	23.	D	33.	A
4.	B	14.	C	24.	A	34.	C
5.	C	15.	D	25.	A	35.	A
6.	A	16.	B	26.	D	36.	B
7.	B	17.	B	27.	D	37.	A
8.	D	18.	A	28.	D	38.	C
9.	B	19.	B	29.	A	39.	C
10.	D	20.	A	30.	C	40.	B

TEST 2

DIRECTIONS: Each question or incomplete statement is followed by several suggested answers or completions. Select the one that BEST answers the question or completes the statement. *PRINT THE LETTER OF THE CORRECT ANSWER IN THE SPACE AT THE RIGHT.*

1. In order to assist his subordinates to advance in the civil service system, a custodial foreman should 1.____

    A. teach them as much as he can about their jobs
    B. put them in charge of a group and let them sink or swim
    C. tell them to read THE CHIEF/CIVIL SERVICE LEADER
    D. reduce their assigned work load by 50 percent so that they can study for a promotion exam

2. A custodial foreman scheduled the thorough cleaning of the swimming pool to take place during the last week of the students' summer vacation period.
   This planning was 2.____

    A. *good,* because the pool will be clean when the students return for the fall semester
    B. *good,* because the pool can be cleaned in an hour or two at any time
    C. *bad,* because if for some reason the job cannot be done on schedule, there is no time left in which to do it before the fall semester starts
    D. *bad,* because the pool should not be cleaned during summer vacation

3. Of the following, the MOST important reason for giving each cleaner a written schedule of the routine daily tasks he is to perform is that it 3.____

    A. relieves the supervisor of responsibility for the routine work
    B. tells the cleaner in detail how to do the work
    C. relieves the supervisor of the job of inspecting the building each day
    D. tells the cleaner what he is expected to do each day

4. Poor planning is indicated by failure to clean several rooms one night because 4.____

    A. several cleaners were sick
    B. of a blackout
    C. the water main burst
    D. delivery of the cleaning supplies was delayed two days

5. The LEAST probable benefit to be derived from a good training program for custodial workers is that 5.____

    A. a higher standard of cleanliness will be attained
    B. productivity will increase
    C. materials will be saved
    D. the poorest worker will be equal to the most highly skilled worker

6. Of the following, the MAIN advantage of training groups of people rather than giving individual instruction is that 6.____

    A. everyone will obtain the same benefit from the training
    B. no one will feel *left out*

35

C. everyone will be given the same information at the same time
D. no further individual instruction will be necessary

7. Plans for a training session for a group of custodial workers should include requests for training films and training aids which are obtainable free of charge from the

   A. cleaning material manufacturers
   B. Museum of Art
   C. department of personnel
   D. budget bureau

8. The first step in the procedure for instructing an employee is to prepare the worker to receive the instruction.
   This preparation should NOT include

   A. putting the employee at ease
   B. asking him what he already knows about the job
   C. placing him in the right location to see your demonstration
   D. having him do the job first and then showing him what he did wrong

9. A cleaner was injured while attempting to carry a floor scrubbing machine up a short stairway.
   In order to prevent this type accident, a custodial foreman should order his cleaners to

   A. keep the scrubbing machines on the ground floor
   B. stop using the machines until he can buy lightweight models
   C. get another cleaner to help lift the machines when necessary
   D. continue lifting the machines without help, since no one was ever previously hurt

10. Before lifting a heavy box from the floor to a table, an employee should

    A. raise one side of the box slightly to determine whether he can lift it alone
    B. get a scale and weigh the box to determine whether he can lift it alone or not
    C. ask the foreman whether it is too heavy to lift alone
    D. get someone to help lift it no matter how heavy it is

11. A custodial foreman in charge of a small group of employees must not only direct the work of the employees assigned to him, but he may also have to do a portion of the manual work himself.
    The tasks he should do are those which

    A. are the simplest
    B. are the most disagreeable
    C. require the most physical strength
    D. require the most skill and experience

12. Of the following statements concerning accidental injury to people at work, the one which is FALSE is

    A. some degree of hazard is associated with every form of activity
    B. people generally have an interest in accident prevention
    C. only the city suffers a monetary loss from accidental injury
    D. every uncontrolled hazard will, in time, produce its share of accidents and injuries

13. The type of fire extinguisher which should NOT be used on an oil fire is the _____ type.   13._____

    A. soda-acid   B. carbon dioxide
    C. foam   D. dry chemical

14. An extension ladder has been placed with its top resting against a wall and its base resting on a concrete floor. The horizontal distance from the wall to the base of the ladder should be _____ of the length of the ladder.   14._____

    A. one-tenth   B. one-quarter
    C. one-half   D. three-quarters

15. The one of the following cleaning tasks which is *also* an important step in fire prevention is   15._____

    A. dusting furniture   B. waxing floors
    C. washing walls   D. clearing away rubbish

16. The two types of fire extinguishers which should be placed in a boiler room which has automatically controlled rotary cup oil burners are   16._____

    A. foam and soda acid
    B. carbon dioxide and loaded stream
    C. carbon dioxide and foam
    D. foam and loaded stream

17. A cleaner tells his foreman, Mr. Black, that the foreman in another building, Mr. White, is teaching a different method of performing a certain cleaning operation and the cleaner thinks Mr. White's method is much better.
    Mr. Black should   17._____

    A. order the cleaner to do it his way or request a transfer
    B. order the cleaner to mind his own business
    C. discuss the operation with Mr. White and try to come to an agreement on the best method
    D. tell his own superior that Mr. White must be doing something wrong

18. The head of the biology department tells the custodial foreman that one of the laboratories was not cleaned properly the night before.
    In response, the custodial foreman should tell the department head   18._____

    A. to report the incident to the superintendent of buildings and grounds
    B. that he will investigate and report back to him promptly
    C. that his cleaners do not like to clean the laboratory
    D. that he cannot get the cleaners to do what he tells them

19. A student complains to a custodial foreman that a cleaner while mopping the floor in the men's lavatory splashed water on the student's shoes.
    The BEST thing for the custodial foreman to do is to   19._____

    A. tell the student the lavatory is closed while it is being mopped and that he had no right to be there
    B. tell the student he will speak to the cleaner and that he is very sorry that it happened

C. call the cleaner into the office and let the student and the cleaner argue
D. smile and ask the student why he is complaining about an old pair of shoes

20. A passer-by suggested a different way of doing a job to a custodial foreman who was supervising a group working on the grounds. The custodial foreman already had tried the suggested method and found it to be too time-consuming. He should tell the passer-by that

A. experienced supervisors have not decided on the best way
B. if he knows so much, he should take the test for custodial foreman
C. he will discuss the suggestion with his superior
D. he has no time to waste listening to half-baked ideas

Questions 21-28.

DIRECTIONS: Questions 21 through 28 are to be answered ONLY in accordance with the following paragraph.

Many custodial foreman have discovered through experience that there are economies to be *realized* by using discretion when ordering items which are similar to each other. For example, it may be cheaper to order a "Sponge block, cellulose, wet size: 6 in. x 4 3/4 in. x *approximately* 34 inches long" at $7.00 than it is to order separate "Sponges, cellulose, wet size: 2 in. x 4 in. x 6 in." at 60 cents. It does not pay to "*over-order*" on floor wax which may turn sour if not used soon enough. An average size college building cannot afford to have extra 30-inch floor brooms costing $19.75 each stored "on the shelf" for a couple of years or to let moths destroy the hair in such brooms if proper safeguards are not used.

21. According to the above passage, the items mentioned which are *similar* are

A. floor brooms   B. sponges
C. floor waxes   D. moths

22. As used in the above paragraph, the term *over-order* means to

A. order again   B. back order
C. order too little   D. order too much

23. Of the items for which prices are given in the above paragraph, the MOST expensive one is the

A. 30 inch floor broom
B. 6 in. x 4 3/4 in. x 34 in. sponge block
C. 2 in. x 4 in. x 6 in. sponge
D. floor wax

24. As used in the above paragraph, the word *realized* means most nearly

A. obtained   B. lost   C. equalized   D. cheapened

25. According to the above paragraph, the one of the following which may be damaged by moths is the

A. floor broom   B. sponge
C. cellulose   D. wool cloth

26. As used in the above paragraph, the term *wet size* means 26.____

    A. the chemical treatment given to sponges
    B. the amount of water the sponge can hold
    C. that the sponges must be kept moist at all times
    D. that the measurements given were taken when the sponges were wet

27. As used in the above paragraph, the word *at* means 27.____

    A. near   B. arrived   C. each   D. new

28. As used in the above paragraph, the word *approximately* means 28.____

    A. exactly   B. about
    C. economical   D. tan

29. A ballast is a part of a(n) 29.____

    A. fluorescent light fixture
    B. electric motor
    C. door bell circuit
    D. incandescent light fixture

30. Most of the lighting circuits in college buildings operate on _____ volts. 30.____

    A. 6   B. 12   C. 120   D. 208

31. An ordinary wall switch which is called a *silent switch* contains a liquid called 31.____

    A. water   B. mercury   C. oil   D. naphtha

32. The rating of the circuit breaker in a lighting circuit is determined by the 32.____

    A. load connected to the circuit
    B. current carrying capacity of the wire
    C. ambient temperature
    D. length of the wire

33. Faucet seats are usually made of 33.____

    A. brass   B. silver   C. lead   D. rubber

34. The BEST way to stop a faucet drip is to 34.____

    A. replace the washer
    B. tighten the faucet handle with a wrench
    C. replace the faucet
    D. clean the trap

35. Of the following, the MOST important step to be taken before starting to operate a steam boiler is to see that the 35.____

    A. water is at proper level
    B. fuel is heated
    C. steam pressure is above 2 psi
    D. vacuum pump is off

36. Of the following hand saws, the one BEST suited for general use when sawing wood is the _____ saw.

    A. band B. jig- C. cross-cut D. rip-

37. The wood MOST generally used for classroom floors is

    A. balsa
    B. teak
    C. mahogany
    D. hard maple

38. The nails USUALLY used to attach wooden molding are known as _____ nails.

    A. cut
    B. finishing
    C. common
    D. flat-head

39. Of the following, the BEST tool to use to remove a chrome-plated bonnet from a faucet is a(n)

    A. vise-grip plier
    B. open-end wrench
    C. Stillson wrench
    D. chisel

40. A short piece of pipe which is externally threaded at both ends is known as a

    A. nipple B. spacer C. coupling D. union

KEY (CORRECT ANSWERS)

1. A	11. D	21. B	31. B
2. C	12. C	22. D	32. B
3. D	13. A	23. A	33. A
4. D	14. B	24. A	34. A
5. D	15. D	25. A	35. A
6. C	16. C	26. D	36. C
7. A	17. C	27. C	37. D
8. D	18. B	28. B	38. B
9. C	19. B	29. A	39. B
10. A	20. C	30. C	40. A

EXAMINATION SECTION
TEST 1

DIRECTIONS: Each question or incomplete statement is followed by several suggested answers or completions. Select the one that BEST answers the question or completes the statement. *PRINT THE LETTER OF THE CORRECT ANSWER IN THE SPACE AT THE RIGHT.*

1. A treated mop is one that has been treated with a mixture of kerosene and oil so that the mop can be *more effectively* used for

    A. wet or damp mopping linoleum floors
    B. dusting and sweeping waxed wood or linoleum floors
    C. sweeping cement corridors and walks
    D. changing the angle of sweeping

    1.____

2. Reversing the handle of a hair brush occasionally is *desirable* in order to

    A. give equal wear to both sides of the brush
    B. make both sides equally dirty
    C. eliminate frequent cleaning of the brush
    D. change the angle of sweeping

    2.____

3. The MOST practical time to sweep classroom floors is

    A. in the morning before students come to school
    B. at noontime
    C. after the close of the afternoon session
    D. between classes during the day

    3.____

4. The substance which is LEAST effective in reducing slipping on icy walks in winter is

    A. ashes   B. salt
    C. sand   D. sawdust

    4.____

5. Floors that are *usually* left UNWAXED are those made of

    A. oak   B. asphalt tile
    C. rubber tile   D. cement

    5.____

6. Sweeping compound made of oil-treated sawdust is NOT desirable for asphalt or rubber tile floors *mainly* because the tile will

    A. dry and become brittle
    B. be softened and discolored
    C. be lessened
    D. show a whitish-faded color

    6.____

7. A detergent is a substance MOST commonly used for

    A. mopping
    B. making sweeping compound
    C. polishing
    D. waxing

    7.____

8. The one of the following cleaning agents that will NOT affect rust stains on porcelain is

   A. dilute muriatic acid
   B. vinegar
   C. oxalic acid
   D. linseed oil

9. "Drano" is used for

   A. removing stains from rugs and carpets
   B. opening clogged pipe lines
   C. washing wood floors
   D. removing fingerprints from painted walls

10. Liquid toilet soap is supplied in 5-gallon cans. If each of the twelve toilet rooms in your building uses an average of one quart of toilet soap per month, the amount of cans you should be required to requisite to cover needs for a three month period is

    A. two   B. three   C. four   D. five

11. A corridor is ten feet wide and 210 feet long. If it takes a two-man crew about one hour to mop 5000 square feet, the amount of time required for mopping the corridor is *most nearly*

    A. 30 minutes
    B. 1 hour
    C. 15 minutes
    D. 10 minutes

12. The MOST important reason for setting up a detailed schedule of work for cleaners is that

    A. initiative of employees is stimulated
    B. important items in building maintenance are less likely to be overlooked
    C. employees will become more efficient in their work
    D. the need for regular check of the cleaning operations will be practically eliminated

13. To reduce waste in the use of cleaning tools and equipment, the MOST effective of the following methods is to

    A. require each cleaner to return a worn broom or brush before a new one is issued
    B. insist that all cleaning tools be used for a specified length of time
    C. make sure that cleaning tools are used properly
    D. keep careful records of the issue of cleaning equipment to cleaners

14. Suppose that you find that one of your crew is doing excellent work. The PROPER thing to do is to

    A. give him easier assignments as a reward
    B. praise his work at the earliest opportunity
    C. tell the other cleaners that his man is doing better work than they are doing
    D. say nothing to avoid having the cleaner become conceited

15. To determine the quality of the work of a cleaner assigned to you, the MOST important factor to consider is the

    A. attendance record of the employee
    B. amount of cleaning material used during the year
    C. appearance of the areas assigned to the employee
    D. ability of the employee to handle situations not in the line of duty

16. Suppose a cleaner asks you the reason for a certain cleaning method and you do not know the answer. The MOST suitable reply of those listed below is to

    A. tell the cleaner to ask someone else or to look up the answer in a book on cleaning methods
    B. admit that you do not know the answer, but that you will find it out for him
    C. tell him to follow his routine schedule and not to worry about the question
    D. determine if the cleaner is using his question as an excuse for loafing

16._____

17. Suppose your superior has given orders for a change in some of the work schedules of your crew. Your men complain to you about these changes.
The PROPER thing to do is to

    A. tell the cleaners to complain to your superior, not to you
    B. advise the men that nothing can be done, even if the complaints are correct
    C. inform the cleaners that the changes were not good and that you did not like them
    D. tell the men that you will take up their complaints with your superior

17._____

18. Before a foreman instructs a new cleaner in his work, he must, as his FIRST step,

    A. decide what must be done to teach the new man
    B. determine if the man is capable of doing the work
    C. see that all cleaners' equipment and supplies to be used by the cleaner are in order and ready
    D. discuss cleaning methods with the cleaner

18._____

19. A cleaner has been transferred to your crew from another building where he has had difficulty with his foreman. When the cleaner reports for work, you should

    A. immediately tell him that he had better toe the mark and follow the instructions given to him
    B. call the foreman in the other building and ask him about the work and attitude of the cleaner
    C. tell the cleaner that to avoid any difficulties in this building, he is not to discuss his problems in the other building with the cleaners in his crew
    D. avoid discussing anything with the cleaner other than to give him his cleaning assignments

19._____

20. A cleaner has come late to work on several occasions. The foreman should

    A. ignore the lateness if the cleaner is superior in his work
    B. recommend suspension of the cleaner for persistent lateness
    C. assign less desirable assignments to the cleaner
    D. discuss the matter with the cleaner before taking any action

20._____

21. When it is necessary for a foreman to have some men work overtime, the BEST approach to the men is to

    A. apologize for the necessity of having them work overtime
    B. advise them that they were selected only because they are considered better workers
    C. tell them that the order came from your superior and was not your fault
    D. explain why overtime was necessary at this time

21._____

22. After you have shown a cleaner how to do a new job, the BEST follow-up step to take is to

    A. watch him carefully whenever he does this job
    B. ask him from time to time how he is getting along
    C. check from time to time the performance of this job
    D. ask another experienced cleaner to check the man's work

23. A cleaner claims that he has been assigned more work than other cleaners in his crew. Your review of the work schedules shows his complaint is justified.
    The MOST appropriate action to take is to

    A. reduce the cleaner's work load slightly to eliminate future complaints
    B. exchange his schedule with that of another cleaner
    C. advise him that your check shows no unfairness in assignments
    D. tell him not to worry about the work given to other cleaners

24. A cleaner complains that the area required to be cleaned in a standard working day is too great. As a result, he is unable to do as good a job as he wants to.
    The foreman should

    A. refer to the schedule and state that it is based on practical study of the work
    B. tell the cleaner that there is no complaint about the quality of his work
    C. go over the cleaner's schedule with him to determine the basis for the complaint
    D. point out that other cleaners have been doing the same amount of work without complaint

25. The one of the following qualities which makes a foreman respected by his cleaners is that he is

    A. easy to confide in
    B. fair in all decisions
    C. easy to please
    D. of a good disposition

26. One of your cleaners disappears from his assignments and is found in an intoxicated condition. Your IMMEDIATE action should be to

    A. send him to the locker room to stay until he is sober enough to work
    B. tell him he is suspended until notified to return to work
    C. send him home for the remainder of the day
    D. assign him to some unimportant job and report the matter to your superior

27. Suppose you have criticized a cleaner for making the error of leaving a pail in a corridor and you find later that he was actually correct in denying that he was at fault.
    It is MOST desirable for you to

    A. apologize to the man for making the mistake
    B. make no apology, but give him preferred assignment
    C. attempt to justify the criticism because the cleaner had been negligent previously
    D. apologize to the cleaner in front of the entire crew

28. Of the following, the MOST important reason for investigating the cause of an accident is to   28.____

   A. determine if the employee injured was at fault
   B. prevent occurence of the accident again
   C. determine if the injured employee deserves compensation
   D. impress on employees the need to be safety-minded

29. In filling out an accident report on a cleaner who was injured, the LEAST important item to cover in the report is the   29.____

   A. attitude of the cleaner towards his job
   B. nature and extent of the injury
   C. work being done by the cleaner when injured
   D. equipment being used when the injury occurred

30. A precaution that should be observed in the care and maintenance of the soda-acid fire extinguisher is: 30.____

   A. It should be hung where it will be protected against freezing.
   B. It should be recharged every month to make sure that the soda and acid do not lose their strength.
   C. It should be hung on brackets at least ten feet above the floor.
   D. The acid bottle should be tightly stoppered to prevent accidental escape of acid.

31. When a soda-acid fire extinguisher is used to put out a small fire, the PROPER procedure in using it is to   31.____

   A. open the valve at the top to enable the water to enter the hose
   B. shake the extinguisher vigorously before directing the water on the fire
   C. pump the handle two or three times before directing the extinguisher
   D. turn the extinguisher upside down and then direct the hose towards the fire

32. The purpose of fire doors in a building is to   32.____

   A. prevent fires
   B. prevent spread of fires
   C. avoid panic
   D. prevent arson

QUESTIONS 33-35.

Questions 33 to 35 refer to the paragraph below:

   Whether a main lobby or upper corridor requires scrubbing or mopping and whether it should be done nightly or less frequently depends on the nature of the floor surface and the amount of traffic. In a building with heavy traffic, it may be desirable every night to scrub the main lobby and to mop the upper floor corridors. In such cases, it may also be found desirable to scrub the upper floors once a week. If traffic is light, it may be only necessary to mop the main lobby every other night and to mop the upper floor corridors once a week. If there is any traffic or usage at all, it will be necessary to at least sweep the corridors nightly.

33. According to this paragraph, in a building with light traffic, the upper floors corridors should be

   A. swept every other night
   B. mopped every night
   C. swept nightly
   D. mopped every other night

34. According to this paragraph, the number of times a floor is cleaned depends

   A. mainly on the type of floor surface
   B. mainly on the type of traffic
   C. only on the amount of traffic
   D. on both the floor surface and amount of traffic

35. According to this paragraph, it may be desirable to have a heavily used main lobby

   A. swept daily and scrubbed weekly
   B. swept daily and mopped weekly
   C. swept and mopped weekly
   D. swept and scrubbed daily

36. Suppose a cleaner tells you that in one of the offices that he was cleaning, he found a number of letters on top of a letter file cabinet. He asks you what he should do with the letters.
   You should tell him to

   A. put the letters on a desk near the cabinet
   B. place the letters in the file cabinet
   C. leave the letters where they are
   D. examine the letters to see it they belong in this office

37. If your superior tells you that the brass door fixtures of a number of rooms have not been properly maintained, the MOST desirable reply to make to your superior is to

   A. advise your superior that the cleaner assigned was not reliable and will be checked carefully in the future
   B. accept the complaint and assure your superior that you will see that the fixtures are maintained properly in the future
   C. reply that because you are shorthanded this week you cannot cover all parts of the cleaning schedule
   D. tell your superior that you will fix these fixtures yourself so that there will be no basis for complaint in the future

38. The one of the following which a foreman should refer to his superior for decision or action is

   A. request of a department official to use some of your crew to move some file cabinets
   B. rotation of assignments of cleaners in his crew

C. a cleaner who has been late on several occasions
D. preparation of accidents report forms covering an accident in which one of his cleaners was involved

39. Suppose you are given a complaint stating that one of the offices is not cleaned properly. The FIRST thing to do in handling the complaint is to

   A. talk to the cleaner to whom this office is assigned
   B. post the complaint on the employee's bulletin board
   C. inspect the office one evening shortly after it has been cleaned
   D. recommend disciplinary action against the cleaner assigned to clean this office

40. A cleaner accidentally hits a bottle of ink, causing a heavy stain on the linoleum floor. After removing as much of the stain as possible, a noticeable discoloration remains. After the cleaner has reported the matter to his foreman, the PROPER step to be taken is to

   A. have the cleaner report to the person in charge of that office to explain what happened
   B. avoid reporting the matter further, but attempt to remove the stain the following day or evening
   C. have the matter discussed by the custodian or foreman with the occupant of that office
   D. have the cleaner apologize to the office occupants and promise to clean or replace the floor covering

KEY (CORRECT ANSWERS)

1.	B	11.	A	21.	D	31.	D
2.	A	12.	B	22.	C	32.	B
3.	C	13.	C	23.	C	33.	C
4.	D	14.	B	24.	C	34.	D
5.	D	15.	C	25.	B	35.	D
6.	B	16.	B	26.	C	36.	C
7.	A	17.	D	27.	A	37.	B
8.	D	18.	A	28.	B	38.	A
9.	B	19.	D	29.	A	39.	C
10.	A	20.	D	30.	A	40.	C

EXAMINATION SECTION
TEST 1

DIRECTIONS: Each question or incomplete statement is followed by several suggested answers or completions. Select the one that BEST answers the question or completes the statement. *PRINT THE LETTER OF THE CORRECT ANSWER IN THE SPACE AT THE RIGHT.*

1. Two cleaners swept four corridors in 24 minutes. Each corridor measured 12 feet x 176 feet.
   The space swept per man per minute was MOST NEARLY _____ square feet.

   A. 50   B. 90   C. 180   D. 350

   1._____

2. The BEST time of the day to dust classroom furniture and woodwork is

   A. in the morning before the students arrive
   B. during the morning recess
   C. during the students' lunch time
   D. immediately after the students are dismissed for the day

   2._____

3. A custodian-engineer wishes to order sponges in the most economical manner. Keeping in mind that large sponges can be cut up into many smaller sizes, the one of the following that has the LEAST cost per cubic inch of sponge is

   A. 2" x 4" x 6" sponges @ $0.24
   B. 4" x 8" x 12" sponges @ $1.44
   C. 4" x 6" x 36" sponges @ $4.80
   D. 6" x 8" x 32" sponges @ $9.60

   3._____

4. Many new products are used in new schools for floors, walls, and other surfaces. A custodian-engineer should determine the BEST procedure to be used to clean such new surfaces by

   A. referring to the Board of Education's manual of procedures
   B. obtaining information on the cleaning procedure from the manufacturer
   C. asking the advice of the mechanics who installed the new material
   D. asking the district supervisor how to clean the surfaces

   4._____

5. The one of the following chemicals that a custodian-engineer should tell a cleaner to use to remove mildew from terazzo is

   A. ammonia   B. oxalic acid
   C. sodium hypochlorite D. sodium silicate

   5._____

6. The type of soft floor that is basically a mixture of oxidized linseed oil, resin, and ground cork pressed upon a burlap backing is known as

   A. asphalt tile   B. cork tile
   C. linoleum   D. vinyl tile

   6._____

7. The difficulty of cleaning soil from surfaces is LEAST affected by the

   A. length of time between cleanings
   B. chemical nature of the soil

   7._____

49

C. smoothness of the surface being cleaned
D. standard time allotted to the job

8. The one of the following cleaning agents that is generally classified as an alkaline cleaner is

   A. sodium carbonate
   B. ground silica
   C. kerosene
   D. lemon oil

9. The one of the following cleaning agents that should be used ONLY when adequate ventilation and protective measures have been taken is

   A. methylene chloride
   B. sodium chloride
   C. sodium carbonate
   D. calcium carbonate

10. Of the following, the MOST important consideration in the selection of a cleaning agent is the

    A. cost per pound or gallon
    B. amount of labor involved in its use
    C. wording of the manufacturer's warranty
    D. length of time the manufacturer has been producing cleaning agents

11. The fan motor in a central vacuum cleaner system is found to be operating at 110% of its rated capacity.
    The one of the following actions which is MOST likely to DECREASE the load on the motor is

    A. tying back several outlets in the open position on each floor
    B. moving the butterfly damper slightly toward the closed position
    C. removing ten percent of the filter bags
    D. operating the bag shaker continuously

12. The one of the following cleaning agents that should be used to remove an accumulation of grease from a concrete driveway is a(n)

    A. acid cleaner
    B. alkaline cleaner
    C. liquid soap
    D. solvent cleaner

13. The instructions for mixing a powdered cleaner in water state that you should mix three ounces of powder in a 14-quart pail three-quarters full of water.
    To obtain a mixture of EQUAL strength in a mop truck containing 28 gallons of water requires _____ ounces of powder.

    A. 6   B. 8   C. 24   D. 32

14. A resin-base floor finish USUALLY

    A. gives the highest lustre of all floor finishes
    B. should be applied in one heavy coat
    C. provides a slip-resistant surface
    D. should not be used on asphalt tile

15. The one of the following cleaning operations of soft floors that generally requires MOST   15.____
    NEARLY the SAME amount of time per 1,000 square feet as damp mopping is

    A. applying a thin coat of wax
    B. sweeping
    C. dust mopping
    D. wet mopping

16. Of the following cleaning jobs, the one that should be allowed the MOST time to com-   16.____
    plete a 1,000 square foot area is

    A. vacuuming carpets
    B. washing painted walls
    C. stripping and waxing soft floors
    D. machine-scrubbing hard floors

17. Of the following, the MOST common use of sodium silicate is to   17.____

    A. seal concrete floors   B. condition leather
    C. treat boiler water   D. neutralize acid wastes

18. Cleaners should be instructed that dust mopping is LEAST appropriate for removing light   18.____
    soil from _____ floors.

    A. terrazzo floors   B. unsealed concrete
    C. resin-finished soft   D. sealed wood

19. Of the following, the substance that should be recommended for polishing hardwood fur-   19.____
    niture is

    A. lemon oil polish   B. neat's-foot oil
    C. paste wax   D. water-emulsion wax

20. The use of concentrated acid to remove stains from ceramic tile bathroom floors USU-   20.____
    ALLY results in making the surface

    A. pitted and porous   B. clean and shiny
    C. harder and glossier   D. waterproof

21. Asphalt tile floors should be protected by coating them with   21.____

    A. hard-milled soap   B. water-emulsion wax
    C. sodium metaphosphate   D. varnish

22. Of the following, the BEST way to economize on cleaning tools and materials is to   22.____

    A. train the cleaners to use them properly
    B. order at least a three-year supply of every item in order to avoid annual price
       increases
    C. attach a price sticker to every item so that the people using them will realize their
       high cost
    D. delay ordering material for three months at the beginning of each year to be sure
       that the old material is used to the fullest extent

23. The MINIMUM amount of free chlorine that swimming pool water should contain for proper disinfection is _____ parts per million.

    A. 1.0   B. 10   C. 50   D. 500

24. The point at which swimming pool filters should be back-washed is when the difference between the inlet and outlet pressures exceeds _____ psi.

    A. 5   B. 10   C. 15   D. 20

25. An orthtolidine test is used to test a water sample to see what quantity it contains of

    A. alum   B. ammonia   C. chlorine   D. soda ash

26. The IDEAL flue gas temperature in a rotary-cup oil-fired boiler should be equal to the steam temperature plus

    A. 50° F   B. 125° F   C. 275° F   D. 550° F

27. The carbon dioxide reading in a boiler flue when the boiler is operating efficiently should be MOST NEARLY

    A. 0.5 inches of water
    B. 8 ounces per mol
    C. 10 psi
    D. 12 percent

28. The one of the following that PRIMARILY indicates a low water level in a steam boiler is the

    A. pressure gauge
    B. gauge glass
    C. safety valve
    D. hydrometer

29. The one of the following steps that should be taken FIRST if a safety valve on a coal-fired steam boiler pops off is to

    A. add water to the boiler
    B. reduce the draft
    C. tap the side of the safety valve with a mallet
    D. open the bottom blow-off valve

30. A device that operates to vary the resistance of an electrical circuit is USUALLY part of a _____ pressurtrol.

    A. high-limit
    B. low-limit
    C. manual-reset
    D. modulating

KEY (CORRECT ANSWERS)

1.	C	16.	C
2.	A	17.	A
3.	B	18.	B
4.	B	19.	C
5.	C	20.	A
6.	C	21.	B
7.	D	22.	A
8.	A	23.	A
9.	A	24.	B
10.	B	25.	C
11.	B	26.	B
12.	D	27.	D
13.	D	28.	B
14.	C	29.	B
15.	A	30.	D

TEST 2

DIRECTIONS: Each question or incomplete statement is followed by several suggested answers or completions. Select the one that BEST answers the question or completes the statement. *PRINT THE LETTER OF THE CORRECT ANSWER IN THE SPACE AT THE RIGHT.*

1. A solenoid valve is actuated by

    A. air pressure
    B. electric current
    C. temperature change
    D. light rays

2. A sequential draft control on a rotary-cup oil-fired boiler should operate to

    A. *open* the automatic damper at the end of the post-purge period
    B. *open* the automatic damper when the draft has increased during normal burner operation
    C. *close* the automatic damper just before the burner motor starts up
    D. *close* the automatic damper after the burner goes off and the burner cycle is completed

3. The one of the following components of flue gas that indicates, when present, that more excess air is being supplied than is being used is

    A. carbon dioxide
    B. carbon monoxide
    C. nitrogen
    D. oxygen

4. An ADVANTAGE that a float-thermostatic steam trap has over a float-type steam trap of comparable rating is that a float-thermostatic trap

    A. requires less maintenance
    B. is easier to install
    C. allows non-condensable gases to escape
    D. releases the condensate at a higher temperature

5. A pump delivers 165 pounds of water per minute against a total head of 100 feet. The water horsepower of this pump is _____ HP.

    A. 1/2   B. 2   C. 5   D. 20

6. Of the following, the BEST instrument to use to measure over-the-fire draft is the

    A. Bourdon tube gauge
    B. inclined manometer
    C. mercury manometer
    D. potentiometer

7. The temperature of the water in a steam-heated domestic hot water tank is controlled by a(n)

    A. aquastat
    B. thermostatic regulating valve
    C. vacuum breaker
    D. thermostatic trap

8. The one of the following conditions that will MOST likely cause fuel oil pressure to fluctuate is

   A. a faulty pressure gauge
   B. a clean oil-strainer
   C. cold oil in the suction line
   D. an over-tight pump drive belt

9. The cooler in a Freon 12 refrigeration system that is equipped with automatic protective devices is MOST likely to be accidentally damaged by water freeze-up when the system('s)

   A. is operating at reduced load
   B. is operating at rated load
   C. condenser water-flow is interrupted
   D. is being pumped down

10. The capacity of a water-cooled condenser is LEAST affected by the

    A. water temperature
    B. refrigerant temperature
    C. surrounding air temperature
    D. quantity of condenser water being circulated

11. Of the following chemicals used in boiler feedwater treatment, the one that should be used to retard corrosion in the boiler circuit due to dissolved oxygen is sodium

    A. aluminate   B. carbonate   C. phosphate   D. sulfite

12. The heating system in a certain school is equipped with vacuum-return condensate pumps.
    The MOST likely place for an air-vent valve to be installed in this plant is on

    A. each radiator
    B. the outlet of the domestic hot-water steam heating coil
    C. the pressure side of the vacuum pump
    D. the shell of the domestic hot water tank

13. *Priming* of a steam boiler is NOT caused by

    A. load swings
    B. uneven fire distribution
    C. too high a water level
    D. high alkalinity of the boiled water

14. A Hartford loop is used in school heating systems PRIMARILY to

    A. provide for thermal expansion of the steam distribution piping
    B. equalize the water level in two or more boilers
    C. prevent siphoning of water out of the boiler
    D. by-pass the electric fuel-oil heaters when the steam heaters are operating

15. Of the following, the MOST likely use for temperature-indicating crayons by a custodian-engineer is in

    A. checking the operation of the radiator traps
    B. replacing room thermometers that have been vandalized
    C. indicating possible sources of spontaneous combustion
    D. checking the effectiveness of an insulating panel

16. A stop-and-waste cock is GENERALLY used on

    A. refrigerant lines between the compressor and the condenser
    B. soil lines
    C. gas supply lines
    D. water lines subjected to low temperatures

17. A pressure regulating valve in a compressed air line should be PRECEDED by a(n)

    A. check valve
    B. intercooler
    C. needle valve
    D. water-and-oil separator

18. A house trap is a fitting placed in the house drain immediately inside the foundation wall of a building.
    The MAIN purpose of a house trap is to

    A. prevent the entrance of sewer gas into the building drainage system
    B. provide access to the drain lines in the basement for cleaning
    C. drain the basement in case of flooding
    D. maintain balanced air pressure in the fixture traps

19. The one of the following that is BEST to use to smooth a commutator is

    A. number 1/0 emery cloth
    B. number 00 sandpaper
    C. number 2 steel wool
    D. a safe edge file

20. The electric service that is provided to most schools in the city is nominally

    A. 208 volt-3 phase - 4 wire - 120 volts to ground
    B. 208 volt-3 phase - 3 wire - 208 volts to ground
    C. 220 volt-2 phase - 3 wire - 110 volts to ground
    D. 440 volt-3 phase - 4 wire - 240 volts to ground

21. All the fuses in an electrical panel are good but the clips on the fuse in circuit No. 1 are much hotter than the clips of the other fuses.
    Of the following, the MOST likely cause of this condition is that

    A. circuit No. 1 is greatly overloaded
    B. circuit No. 1 is carrying much less than rated load
    C. the room temperature is abnormally high
    D. the fuse in circuit No. 1 is very loose in its clips

22. Of the following, the BEST tool to use to drive a lag screw is a(n)

    A. open-end wrench
    B. Stillson wrench
    C. screwdriver
    D. allen wrench

23. Of the following, the one that is MOST likely to be used in landscaping work as ground cover is

    A. barberry
    B. forsythia
    C. pachysandra
    D. viburnum

24. The velocity of air in a ventilation duct is USUALLY measured with a(n)

    A. hydrometer
    B. psychrometer
    C. pyrometer
    D. pitot tube

25. The motor driving a centrifugal pump through a direct-connected flexible coupling burned out.
    When a new motor is ordered, it is IMPORTANT to specify the same NEMA frame size so that the

    A. horsepower will be the same
    B. speed will be the same
    C. conduit box will be in the same location
    D. mounting dimensions will be the same

26. A custodian-engineer should inspect the school building for safety

    A. at least once each day
    B. at least every other day
    C. at least once a week
    D. at the end of each vacation period

27. Of the following, the MOST important practice to follow in order to prevent fires in a school is to train the staff to

    A. fight fires of every kind
    B. detect and eliminate every possible fire hazard
    C. keep halls, corridors, and exits clear
    D. place flammables in fire-proof container

28. The one of the following types of portable fire extinguishers that is MOST effective in fighting an oil fire is the _____ type.

    A. soda-acid
    B. loaded-stream
    C. foam
    D. carbon dioxide

29. A custodian-engineer opens the door to the boiler room and discovers that fuel oil has leaked onto the floor and caught fire.
    Of the following, the FIRST action he should take is to

    A. notify the principal
    B. notify the Fire Department
    C. turn off the remote control switch
    D. fight the fire using a Class B extinguisher

30. The MINIMUM noise level beyond which hearing may be impaired is _____ decibels.

    A. 10
    B. 50
    C. 90
    D. 130

KEY (CORRECT ANSWERS)

1.	B	16.	D
2.	D	17.	D
3.	D	18.	A
4.	C	19.	B
5.	A	20.	A
6.	B	21.	D
7.	B	22.	A
8.	C	23.	C
9.	D	24.	D
10.	C	25.	D
11.	D	26.	A
12.	B	27.	B
13.	D	28.	C
14.	C	29.	C
15.	A	30.	C

EXAMINATION SECTION
TEST 1

DIRECTIONS: Each question or incomplete statement is followed by several suggested answers or completions. Select the one that BEST answers the question or completes the statement. *PRINT THE LETTER OF THE CORRECT ANSWER IN THE SPACE AT THE RIGHT.*

1. Of the following, the BEST practice to follow in criticizing the work performance of a cleaner is to
    A. save up several criticisms and make them all at once
    B. soften your criticisms by being humorous
    C. have another cleaner, who has more seniority, give the criticism
    D. make sure that you explain to the cleaner the reasons for your criticisms

    1.____

2. A group of students complains to you about the lack of cleanliness in the building. You realize that budget cutbacks have unavoidably led to shortages in manpower and equipment for the cleaning staff.
    Of the following, the BEST way for you to answer these students is to
    A. tell them frankly that the cleanliness of the building is none of their business
    B. apologize for the condition of the building and promise that your men will work harder
    C. tell them to take their complaints to the administration and not to you
    D. explain the reason for the building's condition and what you are doing to improve it

    2.____

3. Your supervisor has ordered you to announce to your cleaners a new cleaning rule with which you disagree.
    You should
    A. admit honestly to your cleaners that you disagree with the rule
    B. announce the rule to your cleaners without expressing your disagreement
    C. encourage your cleaners by telling them that you agree with the rule
    D. tell your supervisor that you refuse to announce any rule with which you disagree

    3.____

4. The preparation of work schedules for custodial employees and the daily work routine of these employees is determined and regulated by the
    A. principal   B. district supervisor of custodians
    C. chief of custodians D. school custodian

    4.____

5. The records and reports of school plant operations are originated by the school custodian and forwarded on a monthly basis to the
    A. borough supervisor   B. district superintendent
    C. director of plant operations D. chief of custodians

    5.____

6. The operation, care, maintenance, and minor repair of a school building and grounds is the duty and responsibility of the school custodian.
   This responsibility
   A. can be delegated to the custodial staff
   B. is shared with the custodial staff
   C. cannot be delegated and is the school custodian's only
   D. is shared with the district supervisor

7. A cleaner does a very good job on the work assigned to him, but on several occasions you find him lounging and reading a magazine in an isolated part of the building.
   The BEST thing for you to do is
   A. tell the man to increase the time it takes to do the job so as to reduce his lax time
   B. give him a strong reprimand
   C. check the log book or personnel records and confer with the staff and principal to see if there are any complaints against him
   D. tell the man to report to you whenever he finishes the required work

8. If one of your employees approaches you with a suggestion on how to improve work procedures, you should
   A. ignore it
   B. listen to the suggestion and take appropriate action
   C. refer the employee to the principal
   D. tell the employee to tell the union

9. When instructing a new employee, you should include all of the following EXCEPT
   A. the shortcomings, failures, and attitudes of fellow workers
   B. unusual situations and hazardous conditions of work assignments
   C. the normal hours of employment and special situations which require overtime
   D. the rules, regulations, customs, and policies of the assignment

10. You are newly assigned to a building in which the custodial staff has been working effectively for many years.
    In order to obtain the respect of the staff, you should
    A. immediately make major significant changes in procedures to establish your authority
    B. immediately make minor changes to show that you have new ideas, plans, and organizational ability
    C. criticize your predecessor to establish your identity, attitude, and authority
    D. make no changes to work schedules or assignments until you are fully aware of the existing practices, schedules or assignments

11. Suppose that a cleaner has been found to be quite negligent in his work and has been warned repeatedly by you.
    If you find that your warnings have not changed the man's attitude or work habits, the PROPER thing to do is to

A. discharge the employee
B. change his assignment in the school to a less desirable job
C. have a serious talk with the cleaner to find out why he does not do satisfactory work
D. give the cleaner a final warning

12. An after-school play center is in operation in your building. On a particular afternoon, the children in this activity are especially noisy and creating a disturbance.
The FIRST procedure to follow is to
A. notify the day school principal of this situation
B. notify the teacher in charge of this situation
C. pay no attention to this situation and forget about it
D. notify the police

12.____

13. A school custodian is required to submit several types of written reports to his supervisor on a monthly basis. After submitting his monthly reports, a custodian discovers he has made an error.
The CORRECT procedure for the school custodian to follow concerning this matter is to
A. notify the supervisor and have the supervisor correct the error
B. notify the supervisor and request the return of the report so that the custodian can correct the error
C. take no action so that the error may be unnoticed
D. take no action so that the supervisor may find the mistake

13.____

14. New cleaning materials are constantly appearing on the market.
It would be ADVISABLE for the custodian engineer to
A. sample them to determine the cost factor
B. trial test in an operation
C. check materials for product safety
D. all of the above

14.____

15. All vacuum tubes in oil burner programmers, smoke detection devices, and other electronic controls should be changed
A. as needed B. monthly
C. yearly D. every three years

15.____

16. In the event of flame failure, what occurs FIRST?
A. Magnetic oil valve closes. B. Metering valve reduces oil flow.
C. Magnetic gas valve closes. D. Primary air supply is closed.

16.____

17. A burner-mounted vaporstat is a control used in conjunction with proving
A. ignition B. proper oil temperature
C. flame failure D. primary air

17.____

18. Secondary air dampers on a boiler with a rotary cup oil burner are installed PRIMARILY to
    A. measure the flow of air into the furnace
    B. furnish air for atomization
    C. furnish air for combustion
    D. regulate boiler steam pressure

19. In a fully automatic oil burning plant, ignition of fuel oil in the firebox is accomplished by
    A. spark ignition
    B. hand torch
    C. kerosene rags
    D. spark ignition which ignites a gas pilot

20. The purpose of recirculating fuel oil is PRIMARILY to
    A. bring it up to the proper temperature
    B. heat oil in storage tanks
    C. force out air
    D. bring oil up to burner

21. The atomization of the oil in a rotary cup oil burner is PRIMARILY due to
    A. oil pressure
    B. rotary cup only
    C. secondary air
    D. rotary cup and primary air

22. A rotary cup oil burner is started and stopped by means of the
    A. magnetic oil valve
    B. modutrol motor
    C. pressuretrol
    D. vaporstat

23. The fuel oil suction strainer outside the oil storage tanks should be cleaned when
    A. burner flame fluctuates
    B. steam pressure drops
    C. flame failure occurs
    D. a differential in vacuum reading across strainer occurs

24. The LOWEST temperature at which oil gives off sufficient vapors to explode momentarily, when flame is applied, is known as _____ point.
    A. flash   B. fire   C. pour   D. atomization

25. Air/oil ratio in a rotary cup burner is correctly arrived at with the proper setting of the following:
    A. Aquastat, vaporstat, pressurestat
    B. Metering valve, primary air, pressurestat
    C. Metering valve, primary air, secondary air
    D. Aquastat, primary air, secondary air

KEY (CORRECT ANSWERS)

1.	D	11.	A
2.	D	12.	B
3.	B	13.	B
4.	D	14.	D
5.	A	15.	C
6.	C	16.	A
7.	D	17.	D
8.	B	18.	C
9.	A	19.	D
10.	D	20.	A

21.	D
22.	C
23.	D
24.	A
25.	C

TEST 2

DIRECTIONS: Each question or incomplete statement is followed by several suggested answers or completions. Select the one that BEST answers the question or completes the statement. *PRINT THE LETTER OF THE CORRECT ANSWER IN THE SPACE AT THE RIGHT.*

1. The school custodian can help create goodwill and cooperation by the students, faculty, parents, visitors, and the general public through
    A. minding his own business
    B. carrying out his duties diligently
    C. reporting all infractions to the principal
    D. letting his supervisor worry about building operations

   1.____

2. The school custodian has as his responsibility all of the following equipment, EXCEPT
    A. that used for educational and/or culinary purposes
    B. electrical
    C. swimming pool machinery
    D. elevator and sidewalk hoist equipment

   2.____

3. Upon hiring, custodial employees are required to be
    A. x-rayed or tine tested
    B. fingerprinted and police checked
    C. issued ID cards by personnel security
    D. all of the above

   3.____

4. Minor repairs consist of
    A. mechanical adjustment and repacking
    B. clearing minor stoppages and limited glazing
    C. tightening and temporary repairs
    D. all of the above

   4.____

5. Plant operation of the Board of Education is a bureau within the
    A. Division of School Buildings
    B. Office of Design and Construction
    C. Office of Business Affairs
    D. Bureau of Maintenance

   5.____

6. Of the following ways of improving the success of a safety program, the one MOST likely to secure employee acceptance and interest is
    A. frequent inspection
    B. employee participation in the program
    C. posting attractive notices in work areas and employee quarters
    D. frequent meetings of employees at which safe methods are demonstrated

   6.____

7. With regard to supplies, a GOOD procedure is to utilize a daily inventory. The reason for this is that
    A. you are aware of what is on hand at all times
    B. you know if anyone is stealing
    C. it keeps you busy
    D. you can check and see if your employees are working

   7.____

8. A school custodian notices a man in a corridor. This visitor identifies himself as a police officer and states he is observing a student in one of the classes.
The school custodian should
   A. make no further inquiries
   B. ask if the police officer has checked with the school principal
   C. ask for details—the name of the student, reason for observation, etc. —so as to make a log book entry
   D. ask the officer to leave unless he has written permission from the principal

9. In filling out an accident report on an injured cleaner, the LEAST important item to include in the report is the
   A. equipment being used when the injury occurred
   B. attitude of the cleaner towards his job
   C. nature and extent of the injury
   D. work being done when the accident occurred

10. A dispute arises with a cleaner regarding his duties, where he claims the work assigned is *not his job*. After explaining his duties to him and showing him his work schedule, he still refuses to perform the disputed duties.
To resolve this difficulty, you would
   A. fire him for insubordination
   B. notify the school principal
   C. call in the employees' union delegate
   D. call in the district supervisor of custodians

11. A number of pupil injuries have occurred while they were traveling on school stairs. Your inspection shows no defects or inadequacy of lighting.
The MOST desirable step to take to reduce the frequency of these accidents is to
   A. assign a cleaner to each stairway when being used
   B. put up signs warning children to be careful
   C. discuss the matter with the school principal
   D. install better stair lighting and make sure handrails are in perfect order

12. The *fuel and utility* report is a record of fuel and electricity used in a school building.
This report should be sent to the administrative supervisor
   A. daily   B. weekly   C. monthly   D. yearly

13. One of your employees is constantly dissatisfied and is always complaining.
The BEST procedure to follow regarding this man is to
   A. reprimand him and warn him that his conduct is affecting the other employees and that unless he changes his attitude he will be dismissed
   B. reassign him to a job where he will be more closely supervised
   C. discuss in detail his dissatisfaction and determine the cause
   D. supervise him less closely

14. Custodial payroll reports are submitted 14.____
    A. every two weeks   B. every four weeks
    C. monthly   D quarterly

15. An inventor of capital equipment must be filled out 15.____
    A. monthly   B. upon change of custodians
    C. semi-annually   D. yearly

16. School custodians are required to inspect their buildings for fire prevention 16.____
    and fire safety
    A. daily   B. weekly   C. monthly   D. quarterly

17. A contractor working in your building is doing unsatisfactory repair work. 17.____
    You would notify, in writing, the
    A. borough or administrative supervisor
    B. district superintendent
    C. contract compliance division
    D. director of plant operations

18. If one of your employees frequently misplaces cleaning equipment, you would 18.____
    A. notify the borough supervisor
    B. handle the problem yourself
    C. call in the chief of custodians to speak to the employee
    D. tell the principal of the school and ask for action against the employee

19. Safety education of custodial employees is the direct responsibility of the 19.____
    A. school custodian   B. principal
    C. borough supervisor   D. director of plant operations

20. Worker's compensation insurance coverage for custodian employees is 20.____
    provided by all of the following EXCEPT the
    A. board of education   B. union
    C. school custodian   D. school

21. Request for plumbing repair which cannot be performed by the custodial staff 21.____
    are forwarded to the
    A. chief of custodians   B. director of plant operations
    C. borough supervisor   D. plumbing shops

22. The cleaning of electrical distribution panel boxes and switchboards is the 22.____
    responsibility of the
    A. principal   B. school custodian
    C. district supervisor   D. cleaner

23. A parent complains that one of your cleaner used abusive language to him. As the school custodian, you should
    A. reprimand the cleaner
    B. fire the cleaner
    C. investigate the complaint to find out if there is any basis to the allegation
    D. ignore the complaint

23._____

24. Of the following, the LARGEST individual item of custodial expense in operating a school building is generally the cost of
    A. labor
    B. fuel
    C. electricity
    D. elevator services

24._____

25. A telephone caller tells a school custodian that a bomb has been placed in the building and immediately hangs up the phone.
    The FIRST thing the school custodian should do, in the absence of the principal, is to
    A. call the fire department
    B. call the police department
    C. let the principal's subordinate handle it
    D. ignore the call since most threats are hoaxes

25._____

KEY (CORRECT ANSWERS)

1.	B	11.	C
2.	A	12.	C
3.	D	13.	C
4.	D	14.	B
5.	A	15.	D
6.	B	16.	A
7.	A	17.	A
8.	B	18.	B
9.	B	19.	A
10.	A	20.	B

21.	C
22.	B
23.	C
24.	A
25.	B

EXAMINATION SECTION
TEST 1

DIRECTIONS: Each question or incomplete statement is followed by several suggested answers or completions. Select the one that BEST answers the question or completes the statement. *PRINT THE LETTER OF THE CORRECT ANSWER IN THE SPACE AT THE RIGHT.*

1. Of the following, the BEST way for you to make sure that a cleaner understands a spoken order which you have given to him is for you to
    A. ask him to repeat the order in his own words
    B. ask him whether he has understood the order
    C. watch how he begins to follow the order
    D. ask him whether he has any questions about the order

    1.____

2. You have called a meeting with your cleaners to get their suggestions on ways to keep up cleaning standards in spite of budget cutbacks.
   You will MOST likely be successful in encouraging them to participate in the discussion if you
    A. start the meeting by giving the cleaners all your own suggestions first
    B. keep the meeting going by talking whenever the cleaners have nothing to say
    C. get the cleaners to *think out loud* by asking them for their interpretations of the problem
    D. comment on and evaluate the suggestions made by each cleaner immediately after he makes them

    2.____

3. If a custodian knows that rumor being spread by his assistants are false, he should
    A. tell the assistants that the rumors are false
    B. tell the assistants the facts which the rumors have falsified
    C. threaten to discipline any assistant who spreads the rumors
    D. find out which assistant started the rumor and have him suspended

    3.____

4. One of your cleaners tells you in private that he wants to quit his job.
   The FIRST thing you should do in handling this matter is to
    A. ask the cleaner why he wants to quit his job
    B. tell the cleaner to take a few days to think it over
    C. refer the cleaner to the personnel office
    D. try to convince the cleaner not to quit his job

    4.____

5. The MOST important reason why a custodian should seek the suggestions of his cleaners on job-related matters is that the
    A. cleaners generally have greater knowledge of job-related matters than the custodian
    B. cleaners will tend to have a greater feeling of participation in their jobs by making suggestions

    5.____

C. custodians will be able to hold the cleaners responsible for any suggestions he follows
D. custodians can win the respect of his cleaners by showing them the errors in their suggestions

6. Your supervisor has ordered you to announce to your cleaners a new cleaning rule with which you disagree.
   You should
   A. admit honestly to your cleaners that you disagree with the rule
   B. announce the rule to your cleaners without expressing your disagreement
   C. encourage your cleaners by telling them you agree with the rule
   D. tell your supervisor that you refuse to announce any rule with which you disagree

6.____

7. Of the following, the BEST practice to follow in criticizing the work performance of a cleaner is to
   A. save up several criticisms and make them all at one time
   B. soften your criticism by being humorous
   C. have another cleaner, who has more seniority, give the criticism
   D. make sure that you explain to the cleaner the reasons for your criticism

7.____

8. Of the following, the BEST way to reduce unnecessary absences among your cleaners is to
   A. ask your cleaners the reason for their absence every time they are absent
   B. rely entirely on written warnings once every month to cleaners who have been absent too often during the month
   C. have your cleaners make a formal written report to you every time they are absent, explaining the reason for their absence
   D. threaten to fire your cleaners every time they are absent

8.____

9. A group of students complains to you about the lack of cleanliness in your building. You realize that budget cutbacks are unavoidably led to shortages in manpower and equipment for the cleaning staff.
   Of the following, the BEST way for you to answer these students is to
   A. tell them frankly that the cleanliness of the building is none of their business as students
   B. apologize for the condition of the building and promise that your men will work harder
   C. tell them to take their complaints to the administration and not to you
   D. explain the reasons for the building's condition and what you are doing to improve it

9.____

10. The MOST important role of the school custodian in promoting public relations in the community should be to help
    A. increase understanding between the custodial staff and the community which it serves
    B. keep from community attention any failings on the part of the custodial staff

10.____

C. increase the authority of the custodial staff over the community with which it deals
D. keep the community from interfering in the operations of the custodial staff

11. A teacher conducting a class calls you to complain that the cleaners cleaning the empty classroom next to hers are being unnecessarily noisy.
Of the following, the BEST response to the teacher is to tell her that
A. she should go next door to tell the cleaners to stop the unnecessary noise
B. you will tell the cleaners about her complaint and instruct them not to make unnecessary noise
C. she should file a formal complaint against the cleaners with your superior
D. you will come to her classroom to judge for yourself whether the cleaners are being unnecessarily noisy

11.____

12. The attitude a school custodian should generally maintain toward the faculty and students is one of
A. avoidance   B. superiority   C. courtesy   D. servility

12.____

13. The flow of oil in an automatic rotary cup oil burner is regulated by a(n)
A. thermostat
B. metering valve
C. pressure relief valve
D. electric eye

13.____

14. The one of the following devices that is required on both coal-fired and oil-fired boilers is a(n)
A. safety valve
B. low water cut-off
C. feedwater regulator
D. electrostatic precipitator

14.____

15. The type of fuel which must be preheated before it can be burned efficiently is
A. natural gas
B. pea coal
C. number 2 oil
D. number 6 oil

15.____

16. A suction gauge in a fuel-oil transfer system is USUALLY located
A. before the strainer
B. after the strainer and before the pump
C. after the pump and before the pressure relief valve
D. after the pressure relief valve

16.____

17. The FIRST item that should be checked before starting the fire in a steam boiler is the
A. thermostat
B. vacuum pump
C. boiler water level
D. feedwater regulator

17.____

18. Operation of a boiler that has been *sealed* by the Department of Buildings is
A. prohibited
B. permitted when the outside temperature if below 32°F
C. permitted between the hours of 6:00 A.M. and 8:00 A.M. and 9:00 P.M. and 11:00 P.M.
D. permitted only for the purpose of heating domestic water

18.____

19. Lowering the thermostat setting by 5 degrees during the heating season will result in fuel savings of MOST NEARLY _____ percent.
    A. 2   B. 5   C. 20   D. 50

20. An electrically-driven rotary fuel oil pump MUST be protected from internal damage by the installation in the oil line of a
    A. discharge side strainer
    B. check valve
    C. suction gauge
    D. pressure relief valve

21. A float-thermostatic steam trap in a condensate return line that is operating properly will allow
    A. steam and air to pass and will hold back condensate
    B. air and condensate to pass and will hold back steam
    C. steam and condensate to pass and will hold back air
    D. steam to pass and will hold back air and condensate

22. Changes in the combustion efficiency of a boiler can be determined by comparing changes in stack temperature and
    A. steam pressure in the header
    B. over the fire draft
    C. percentage of carbon dioxide
    D. equivalent of direct radiation

23. The classification of the coal that is USUALLY burned in a city school building is
    A. anthracite
    B. bituminous
    C. semi-bituminous
    D. lignite

24. A boiler is equipped with the following pressuretrols:
    I. Manual-reset   II. Modulating   III. High-limit
    The CORRECT sequence in which these devices should be actuated by rising steam pressure is
    A. I, II, III   B. II, III, I   C. III, I, II   D. III, II, I

25. The temperature of the returning condensate in a low-pressure steam heating system if 195°F.
    This temperature indicates that
    A. some radiator traps are defective
    B. some boiler tubes are leaking
    C. the boiler water level is too low
    D. there is a high vacuum in the return line

26. An over-the-fire draft gauge in a natural draft furnace is USUALLY read in
    A. feet per minute
    B. pounds per square inch
    C. inches of mercury
    D. inches of water

27. The Air Pollution Code states that no person shall cause or permit the emission of an air contaminant of a density which appears as dark or darker than number ____ on the standard smoke chart.
    A. one   B. two   C. three   D. four

28. The equipment which is used to provide tempered fresh air to certain areas of a school building is a(n)
    A. exhaust fan
    B. window fan
    C. fixed louvre
    D. heating stack

29. When a glass globe is put back over a newly replaced lightbulb in a ceiling light fixture, the holding screws on the globe should be tightened, then loosened, one half turn.
    This is done MAINLY to prevent
    A. fires caused by electrical short circuits
    B. cracking of the globe due to heat expansion
    C. falling of the globe from the light fixture
    D. building up of harmful gases inside the globe

30. Standard 120 volt type fuses are GENERALLY rated in
    A. farads   B. ohms   C. watts   D. amperes

31. A cleaner informs you that his electric vacuum cleaner is not working even though he tried the off-on switch several times and checked to see that the plug was still in the wall outlet.
    Of the following, the FIRST course of action you should take in this situation is to
    A. determine if the circuit breaker has tripped out
    B. take apart the vacuum cleaner
    C. replace the electric cord on the vacuum cleaner
    D. replace the electrical outlet

32. The one of the following that is the MOST practical method for a school custodian to use in making a temporary repair in a straight portion of a water pipe which has a small leak is to
    A. attach a clamped patch over the leak
    B. weld or braze the pipe, depending on the material
    C. drill and tap the pipe, then insert a plug
    D. fill the hole with an epoxy sealer

33. The PRIMARY function of the packing which is generally found in the stuffing box of a centrifugal pump is to
    A. compensate for misalignment of the pump shaft
    B. prevent leakage of the fluid
    C. control the discharge rate of the pump
    D. provide support for the pump shaft

34. Of the following, the MOST important reason for replacing a worn washer in a dripping faucet as soon as possible is to prevent
    A. overflow of the sink trap
    B. the mixture of hot and cold water in the sink
    C. damage to the faucet parts that can be the result of overtightening the stem
    D. air from entering the supply line

35. In carpentry work, the MOST commonly used hand saw is the _____ saw.   35.____
    A. hack   B. rip   C. buck   D. cross-cut

36. The device which USUALLY keeps a doorknob from rotating on the spindle is a   36.____
    A. cotter pin   B. tapered key
    C. set screw   D. stop screw

37. The following tasks are frequently done when an office is cleaned: 37.____
    I. The floor is vacuumed.
    II. The ashtrays and wastebaskets are emptied.
    III. The desks and furniture are dusted.
    The order in which these tasks should GENERALL be done is
    A. I, II, III   B. II, III, I   C. III, II, I   D. I, III, II

38. When wax is applied to a floor by the use of a twine mop with a handle, the   38.____
    wax should be _____ with the mop.
    A. applied in thin coats
    B. applied in heavy coats
    C. poured on the floor, then spread
    D. dripped on the floor, then spread

39. The BEST way to clean dust from an acoustical type ceiling is with a   39.____
    A. strong soap solution   B. wet sponge
    C. vacuum cleaner   D. stream of water

40. Of the following, the MOST important reason why a wet mop should NOT be   40.____
    wrung out by hand is that
    A. the strings of the mop will be damaged by hand-wringing
    B. sharp objects picked up by the mop may injure the hands
    C. the mop cannot be made dry enough by hand-wringing
    D. fine dirt will become embedded in the strings of the mop

KEY (CORRECT ANSWERS)

1.	A	11.	B	21.	B	31.	A
2.	C	12.	C	22.	C	32.	A
3.	B	13.	B	23.	A	33.	B
4.	A	14.	A	24.	B	34.	C
5.	B	15.	D	25.	A	35.	D
6.	B	16.	B	26.	D	36.	C
7.	D	17.	C	27.	D	37.	B
8.	A	18.	A	28.	B	38.	A
9.	D	19.	C	29.	B	39.	C
10.	A	20.	B	30.	D	40.	B

TEST 2

DIRECTIONS: Each question or incomplete statement is followed by several suggested answers or completions. Select the one that BEST answers the question or completes the statement. *PRINT THE LETTER OF THE CORRECT ANSWER IN THE SPACE AT THE RIGHT.*

1. When a painted wall is washed by hand, the wall should be washed from the _____ with a _____ sponge.   1.____
    A. top down; soaking wet
    B. bottom up; soaking wet
    C. top down; damp
    D. bottom up; damp

2. When a painted wall is brushed with a clean lambswool duster, the duster should be drawn _____ with _____ pressure.   2.____
    A. downward; light
    B. upward; light
    C. downward; firm
    D. upward; firm

3. The one of the following items which BEST describes the size of a floor brush is   3.____
    A. 72 cubic inch
    B. 32 ounce
    C. 24 inch
    D. 10 square foot

4. When a slate blackboard is washed by hand, it is BEST to use   4.____
    A. a mild soap solution and allow the blackboard to air dry
    B. warm water and allow the blackboard to air dry
    C. a mild soap solution and sponge the blackboard dry
    D. warm water and sponge the blackboard dry

5. The MAIN reason why the handle of a reversible floor brush should be shifted from one side of the brush lock to the opposite side is to   5.____
    A. change the angle at which the brush sweeps the floor
    B. give equal wear to both sides of the brush
    C. permit the brush to sweep hard-to-reach areas
    D. make it easier to sweep blackboard

6. When a long corridor is swept with a floor brush, it is good practice to   6.____
    A. push the brush with moderately long strokes and flick it after each stroke
    B. press on the brush and push it the whole length of the corridor in one sweep
    C. pull the brush inward with short, brisk strokes
    D. sweep across rather than down the length of the corrido

7. Of the following office cleaning jobs performed during the year, the one which should be done MOST frequently is   7.____
    A. cleaning the fluorescent lights
    B. dusting the Venetian blinds
    C. cleaning the bookcase glass
    D. carpet-sweeping the rug

8. The BEST polishing agent to use on wood furniture is
   A. pumice
   B. paste wax
   C. water emulsion wax
   D. neatfoot's oil

9. Lemon oil polish is used BEST to polish
   A. exterior bronze
   B. marble walls
   C. lacquered metal floors
   D. leather seats

10. Cleaning with trisodium phosphate will MOST likely damage
    A. toilet bowls
    B. drain pipes
    C. polished marble floors
    D. rubber tile floors

11. Of the following cleaning agents, the one which should NOT be used is
    A. caustic lye
    B. detergent
    C. scouring powder
    D. ammonia

12. The one of the following cleaners which GENERALLY contains an abrasive is
    A. caustic lye
    B. trisodium phosphate
    C. scouring powder
    D. ammonia

13. The instructions on a box of cleaning powder say, *Mix one pound of cleaning powder in four gallons of water.*
    According to these instructions, how many ounces of cleaning powder should be mixed in one gallon of water?
    A. 4   B. 8   C. 12   D. 16

14. In accordance with recommended practice, a dust mop, when not used, should be stored
    A. hanging, handle end down
    B. hanging, handle end up
    C. standing on the floor, handle end down
    D. standing on the floor, handle end up

15. The two types of floors found in public buildings are classified as *hard* and *soft* floors.
    An example of a hard floor is one made of
    A. linoleum   B. cork   C. ceramic tile   D. asphalt tile

16. The BEST way for a custodian to determine whether a cleaner is doing his work well is by
    A. observing the cleaner a work for several hours
    B. asking the cleaner questions about the work
    C. asking other cleaners to rate his work
    D. inspecting the cleanliness of the spaces assigned to the cleaner

17. A chemical frequently used to melt ice on outdoor pavements is
    A. ammonia
    B. soda
    C. carbon tetrachloride
    D. calcium chloride

18. A herbicide is a chemical PRIMARILY used as a(n)
    A. disinfectant B. fertilizer
    C. insect killer D. weed killer

19. Established plants that continue to blossom year after year without reseeding are GENERALLY known as
    A. annuals B. parasites C. perennials D. symbiotics

20. A ferrous sulfate solution is sometimes used to treat shrubs or trees that have a deficiency of
    A. boton B. copper C. iron D. zinc

21. A tree described is deciduous.
    This means PRIMARILY that it
    A. bears nuts instead of fruit B. has been pruned recently
    C. usually grows in swampy ground D. loses its leaves in fall

22. If you are told that a container holds a 20-7-7 fertilizer, it is MOST likely that twenty percent of this fertilizer is
    A. nitrogen B. oxygen
    C. phosphoric acid D. potash

23. When the national flag is in such a worn condition that it is no longer a fitting emblem for display, it should be disposed of by
    A. bagging inconspicuously with other disposables
    B. burning in an inconspicuous place
    C. laundering and then using it for cleaning purposes
    D. storing for future use as a painters dropcloth

24. The landscape drawings for a school indicate the planting of *Acer platanoides* at a certain location on the grounds.
    Acer platanoides is a type of
    A. privet hedge B. rose bush
    C. maple tree D. tulip bed

25. Improper use of a carbon dioxide type portable fire extinguisher may cause injury to the operator because
    A. handling the nozzle during discharge can cause frostbite to the skin
    B. carbon dioxide is highly poisonous if breathed into the lungs
    C. use of carbon dioxide on a oil fire can cause a chemical explosion
    D. of the extremely high pressures inside the extinguisher

26. When using a portable single ladder with ten rungs, the GREATEST number of rungs that a cleaner should climb up is
    A. 7 B. 8 C. 9 D. 10

4 (#2)

27. Of the following types of portable fire extinguishers, the one which should be used to control a fire in or around live electrical equipment is the _____ type.
    A. foam
    B. soda acid
    C. carbon dioxide
    D. gas cartridge water

    27.____

28. The MOST frequent cause of accidental injuries to workers on the job is
    A. unsafe working practices of employees
    B. poor design of buildings and working areas
    C. lack of warning signs in hazardous working areas
    D. lack of adequate safety guards on equipment and machinery

    28.____

29. Of the following, the MOST important purpose of preparing an accident report on an injury to a cleaner is to help
    A. collect statistics on different types of accidents
    B. calm the feelings of the injured cleaner
    C. prevent similar accidents in the future
    D. prove that the cleaner was at fault

    29.____

30. A cleaner is attempting to lift a heavy drum of liquid cleaner from the floor to a shelf at waist height.
    He will MOST likely avoid personal injury in lifting the drum if he
    A. keeps his back as straight as possible and lift the weight
    B. arches his back and lifts the weight primarily with his back muscles
    C. keeps his back as straight as possible and lifts the weight primarily with his leg muscles
    D. arches his back and lifts the weight primarily with his leg muscles

    30.____

31. Of the following, the BEST first aid treatment for a cleaner who has burned his hand with dry caustic lye crystals is to
    A. wash his hand with large quantities of warm water
    B. brush his hand lightly with a soft, clean brush and wrap it in a clean rag
    C. place his hand in a mild solution of ammonia and cool water
    D. wash his hand with large quantities of cold water

    31.____

32. The purpose of the third prong in a three-prong electric plug used on a 120-volt electric vacuum cleaner is to prevent
    A. serious overheating of the vacuum cleaner
    B. electric shock to the operator of the vacuum cleaner
    C. generation of dangerous microwaves by the vacuum cleaner
    D. sparking in the electric outlet caused by a loose electrical wire

    32.____

33. Of the following, the LEAST effective method for a school custodian to use to reduce window glass breakage in his school is to
    A. keep the area near the school free of sticks and stones
    B. consult with parents and civic organizations and request their assistance in reducing breakage

    33.____

C. request that neighbors living near the school report afterhours incidents to the police department
D. develop a reputation as a *tough guy* with the students so that they will be afraid to break windows in the school

34. The one of the following procedures that a school custodian should use when a telephone caller makes a threat to place a bomb in the school is to
    A. hang up on the caller
    B. keep the caller talking as long as possible and make notes on what he says
    C. tell the caller he has the wrong number
    D. tell the caller his voice is being recorded and the call is being traced to its source

35. A school custodian is responsible for enforcing certain safety regulations in the school.
    The MOST important reason for enforcing safety regulations is because
    A. every accident can be prevented
    B. compliance with safety regulations will make all other safety efforts unnecessary
    C. safety regulations are the law and law enforcement is an end in itself
    D. safety regulations are based on reason and experience with the best methods of accident prevention

36. The safety belts that are worn by cleaners when washing outside windows should be inspected
    A. before each use   B. weekly
    C. monthly   D. semi-annually

37. The one of the following actions that a school custodian should take to help reduce burglary losses in the school is to
    A. leave all the lights on in the school overnight
    B. see that interior and exterior doors are securely locked
    C. set booby traps that will severely injure anyone breaking in
    D. set up an apartment in the school basement and stay at the school every night

38. The one of the following types of locks that is used on emergency exit doors is a _____ bolt.
    A. panic   B. dead   C. cinch   D. toggle

39. A telephone caller tells a school custodian that a bomb has been placed in the building and immediately hangs up the phone.
    The FIRST thing the school custodian should do, in the absence of the principal, is to
    A. call the fire department
    B. call the police department
    C. let his subordinate handle it
    D. ignore the call, since most threats are hoaxes

40. If an employee's bi-weekly salary is $1,200.00 and 6.7% is withheld for taxes, the amount to be withheld for this purpose is MOST NEARLY 40._____
    A. $62.00   B. $66.00   C. $82.00   D. $74.00

KEY (CORRECT ANSWERS)

1.	D	11.	A	21.	D	31.	D
2.	A	12.	C	22.	A	32.	B
3.	C	13.	A	23.	B	33.	D
4.	B	14.	B	24.	C	34.	B
5.	B	15.	C	25.	A	35.	D
6.	A	16.	D	26.	B	36.	A
7.	D	17.	D	27.	C	37.	B
8.	B	18.	D	28.	A	38.	A
9.	A	19.	C	29.	C	39.	B
10.	C	20.	C	30.	C	40.	C

EXAMINATION SECTION
TEST 1

DIRECTIONS: Each question or incomplete statement is followed by several suggested answers or completions. Select the one that BEST answers the question or completes the statement. *PRINT THE LETTER OF THE CORRECT ANSWER IN THE SPACE AT THE RIGHT.*

1. A custodian was given a booklet that showed a new work method that could save time. He didn't tell his men because he thought that they would get the booklet anyway. For the custodian to have acted like this is a

    A. *good* idea, because he saves the time and bother of talking to the men
    B. *bad* idea, because he should make sure his men know about better work methods
    C. *good* idea, because the men would rather read about it themselves
    D. *bad* idea, because a supervisor should always show his men every memo he gets from higher authority

1.____

2. A custodian found it necessary to discipline two subordinates. One man had been operating his equipment in a wrong way, while the other man came to work late for three days in a row. The supervisor decided to talk to both men together.
For the custodian to deal with the problems in this way is a

    A. *good* idea, because each man will learn about the difficulties of the other person and how to solve such difficulties
    B. *bad* idea, because the supervisor should wait until he can bring a larger group together and save time in discussing such questions
    C. *good* idea, because he will be able to get the men to see that their problems are related
    D. *bad* idea, because he should meet with each man separately and give him his full attention

2.____

3. A custodian should try to make his men feel their jobs are important in order to

    A. get the men to say good things about their supervisor to his own superior
    B. get the men to think in terms of advancing to better jobs
    C. let higher management in the agency know that the supervisor is efficient
    D. help the men to be able to work more efficiently and enthusiastically

3.____

4. A custodian should know approximately how long it takes to do a particular kind of job CHIEFLY because he

    A. will know how much time to take if he has to do it himself
    B. will be able to tell his men to do it even faster
    C. can judge the performance of the person doing the job
    D. can retrain experienced employees in better work habits

4.____

5. Custodians often get their employees' opinions about better work methods because

    A. the men will know that they are respected
    B. the men would otherwise lose all their confidence in the supervisor
    C. the supervisor might find in this way a good suggestion he could use
    D. this is the best method for improvement of work methods

5.____

6. Right after you have trained your subordinates in doing a new job, you find that they seem to be doing all right, but that it will take them several days to finish. You also have several groups of men working at other locations. The MOST efficient way for you to make sure that the men continue doing the new job properly is to

   A. stay on that job with the men until it is finished, just in case trouble develops
   B. visit the men every half hour until the job is done
   C. stay away from their job that day, and visit the men the next day to ask them if they had any problems
   D. visit the men a few times each day until they finish the new job

7. Assume that one of your new employees is older than you are. You also think that he may be hard to get along with because he is older than you.
   The BEST way for you to avoid any problems with the older worker is for you to

   A. *lay down the law* immediately and tell the man he better not cause you any trouble
   B. treat the man just the way you would any other worker
   C. always ask the older worker for advice in the presence of all the men
   D. ignore the man entirely until he realizes that you are the boss

8. Assume you have tried a new method suggested by one of your employees, and find that it is easier and cheaper than the method you had been using.
   The proper thing for you to do NEXT is to

   A. say nothing to anyone, but train your men to use the new method
   B. train your men to use the new method and tell your crew that you got the idea from one of the men
   C. continue using the old method, because a supervisor should not use suggestions of his men
   D. have your crew learn the new method and take credit for the idea since you are the boss

9. Suppose you are a custodian and your superior tells you that the way your men are doing a certain procedure is wrong and that you should re-train your men as soon as possible. When you begin to re-train the men, the FIRST thing you should do is

   A. tell your men that a wrong procedure had been used and that a new method must be learned as a result
   B. train your employees in the new method with no explanation, since you are the boss
   C. tell the crew that your superior has just decided that everyone should learn a new method
   D. tell the crew that your superior says your method is wrong, but that you don't agree with this

10. It is *bad* practice to criticize a man in front of the other men because

    A. people will think you are too strict
    B. it is annoying to anyone who walks by
    C. it is embarrassing to the man concerned
    D. it will antagonize the other men

11. A custodian decides not to put his two best men on a work detail because he knows that they won't like it.
    For the custodian to make the work assignment this way is a

    A. *good* idea, because it is only fair to give your best men a break once in a while
    B. *bad* idea, because you should treat all of your men fairly and not show favoritism
    C. *good* idea, because you save the strength of these men for another job
    D. *bad* idea, because more of the men should be exempted from the assignment

11.____

12. Suppose you are a custodian and you find it inconvenient to obey an established procedure set by your agency. You think another procedure would be better.
    The BEST thing to do FIRST about this procedure that you don't like is for you to

    A. obey the procedure even if you don't want to, and suggest your idea to your own supervisor
    B. disregard the procedure because a supervisor is supposed to have some privileges
    C. follow the procedure some of the time, but ignore it when the men aren't watching
    D. organize a group of other supervisors to get the procedure changed

12.____

13. A custodian estimated that it would take his crew one workday per week to do a certain job each week. However, after a month he noticed that the job averaged two-and-a-half days a week, and this delayed other jobs that had to be done.
    The FIRST thing that the custodian should do in this case is to

    A. call his men together and warn them that they will get a poor work evaluation if they don't work harder
    B. talk to each man personally, asking him to work harder on the job
    C. go back and study the maintenance job by himself, to see if more men should be assigned to the job
    D. write his boss a report describing in detail how much time it is taking the men to do the job

13.____

14. An employee complains to you that some of his work assignments are too difficult to do alone.
    Which of the following is the BEST way for you to handle this complaint?

    A. Go with him to see exactly what he does and why he finds it so difficult.
    B. Politely tell the man that he has to do the job or be brought up on charges.
    C. Tell the man to send his complaint to the head of your agency.
    D. Sympathize with the man and give him easier jobs.

14.____

15. The BEST way for a custodian to keep control of his work assignments is to

    A. ask the men to report to him immediately when their jobs are finished
    B. walk around the buildings once a week, and get a first-hand view of what is being done
    C. keep his ears open for problems and complaints, but leave the men alone to do the work
    D. write up a work schedule, and check it periodically against the actual work done

15.____

16. A custodian made a work schedule for his men. At the bottom of it he wrote, *No changes or exceptions will be made in this schedule for any reason.*
    For the custodian to have made this statement is

    A. *good,* because the men will respect the custodian for his attitude
    B. *bad,* because there are emergencies and special situations that occur
    C. *good,* because each man will know exactly what is expected of him
    D. *bad,* because the men should expect that no changes will ever be made in the work schedule without written permission

17. Which one of the following would NOT be a result of a well-planned work schedule?
    The schedule

    A. makes efficient use of the time of the staff
    B. acts as a checklist for an important job that might be left out
    C. will give an idea of the work to a substitute supervisor
    D. shows at a glance who the best men are

18. A new piece of equipment you have ordered is delivered. You are familiar with it but the men under you, who will use it, do not know the equipment.
    Of the following methods, which is the BEST to take in explaining to them how to operate this equipment?

    A. Ask the men to watch other crews using the equipment
    B. Show one reliable man how to operate the equipment and ask him to teach the other men
    C. Ask the men to read the instructions in the manual for the equipment
    D. Call the men together and show them how to operate the equipment

19. One custodian assigns work to his men by calling his crew together each week and describing what has to be done that week. He then tells them to arrange individual assignments among themselves and to work as a team during the week.
    This method of scheduling work is a

    A. *good* idea, because this guarantees that the men will work together
    B. *bad* idea, because responsibility for doing the job is poorly fixed
    C. *good* idea, because the men will finish the job in less tirae working together
    D. *bad* idea, because the supervisor should always stay with his men

20. Suppose that a custodial assistant came to the custodian with a problem concerning his assignment.
    For the custodian to listen to this problem is a

    A. *good* idea, because a supervisor should always take time off to talk when one of his men wants to talk
    B. *bad* idea, because the supervisor should not be bothered during the work day
    C. *good* idea, because it's the job of the supervisor to deal with problems of job assignment
    D. *bad* idea, because the employee could start annoying the supervisor with all sorts of problems

21. Suppose that on the previous afternoon you were looking for an experienced employee in order to give him an emergency job and he was missing from his job location. The next morning he tells you that he got sick suddenly and had to go home, but couldn't tell you since you weren't around. He has never done this before.
What should you do?

    A. Tell the man he is excused and that in such circumstances he did the wisest thing.
    B. Bring the man up on charges because, whatever he says, he could still have notified you.
    C. Have the man examined by a doctor to see if he really was sick the day before
    D. Explain to the man that he should make every effort to tell or to get a message to you if he must leave

22. An employee had a grievance and went to the custodian about it. The employee wasn't satisfied with the way the custodian tried to help him, and told him so. Yet the custodian had done everything he could under the circumstances.
The PROPER action for the supervisor to take at this time is to

    A. politely tell the employee that there is nothing more for the custodian to do about the problem
    B. let the employee know how he can bring his complaint to a higher authority
    C. tell the employee that he must solve the problem on his own, since he didn't want to follow the custodian's advice
    D. suggest to the employee that he ask another supervisor for assistance

23. In which of the following situations is it BEST to give your men spoken rather than written orders?

    A. You want your men to have a record of the instructions.
    B. Spoken instructions are less likely to be forgotten.
    C. An emergency situation has arisen in which there is no time to write up instructions.
    D. There are instructions on time and leave regulations which are complicated.

24. One of your employees tells you that a week ago he had a small accident on the job, but he didn't bother telling you because he was able to continue working.
For the employee not to have told the custodian about the accident was

    A. *good,* because the accident was a small one
    B. *bad,* because all accidents should be reported, no matter how small
    C. *good,* because the custodian should be bothered only for important matters
    D. *bad,* because having an accident is one way to get excused for the day

25. For a custodian to deal with each of his subordinates in exactly the same manner is

    A. *poor,* because each man presents a different problem and there is no other way of handling all problems
    B. *good,* because once a problem is handled with one man, he can handle another man with the same problem
    C. *poor,* because the men will resent it if they are not handled each in a better way than others
    D. *good,* because this assures fair and impartial treatment of each subordinate

KEY (CORRECT ANSWERS)

1. B
2. D
3. D
4. C
5. C

6. D
7. B
8. B
9. A
10. C

11. B
12. A
13. C
14. A
15. D

16. B
17. D
18. D
19. B
20. C

21. D
22. B
23. C
24. B
25. A

TEST 2

DIRECTIONS: Each question or incomplete statement is followed by several suggested answers or completions. Select the one that BEST answers the question or completes the statement. *PRINT THE LETTER OF THE CORRECT ANSWER IN THE SPACE AT THE RIGHT.*

1. One day a custodial assistant said to the custodian, *I can get a tile cleaner that is as good as the stuff we use, and for less money, because my brother is a building contractor. How about it?*
   The CORRECT way for the custodian to handle this situation is for him to

   A. thank the assistant, but tell him that individual workers cannot buy their own cleaning material for project use
   B. tell the assistant that no one has any right to start interfering in the buying procedures of the authority
   C. go along with the assistant and buy the cleaner from his brother, because it might save money for the authority
   D. tell the assistant to have his brother contact the project manager

2. A new custodial assistant under your supervision is waxing a floor for the first time. While the job seems to be going along well, he is not doing it quite the way you asked him to do it and so is taking longer than he should. Which of the following is the BEST action for you to take under these conditions?

   A. Leave him to finish the job and go on to the next one
   B. Interrupt him and tell him to do the job the way he was taught
   C. Tell him he is doing well but that he should do better
   D. Explain to him why your way is faster and tell him to try it

3. The easiest way for a custodian to find out how many supplies are available is to

   A. look at last year's figures
   B. keep an up-to-date inventory
   C. ask one of the men to let you know
   D. check the availability when he uses a special item

4. Of the following, the MOST likely result of a report that has been planned well is that it will

   A. explain, in detail, general procedures of supervision
   B. be read by most of the top officials of the department
   C. have some award-winning suggestions
   D. state the facts in a clear, orderly way

5. It is better to make a written report, instead of a face-to-face report, when

   A. you expect your superior to have questions about what is in the report right away
   B. your superior wants to know about your work immediately
   C. the report is very short
   D. you will have to give your report to many people in different locations

6. Of the following, the MOST important fact a custodian should include in an accident report is

   A. the name of the insurance company of the injured person
   B. cost to the city of the accident
   C. name and address of the injured person
   D. your idea for preventing such an accident in the future

7. Making an outline of the contents of a long report, before writing the report, is often a good idea. The advantage is that

   A. you can file an outline to refer to it in the future
   B. your supervisor can see it and know that you are working on the report
   C. you can make the outline a part of your report
   D. it will help you in writing the report

8. Of the following, the MOST important reason for the custodian's making detailed reports in all accidents is to

   A. have a record of who is at fault in case lawsuits should result
   B. be better able to estimate the cost of the accident
   C. reduce the number of compensation claims
   D. determine the cause of the accident and prevent future accidents

9. A custodian's written instructions to his staff on the subject of security in public buildings should include instructions to

   A. exclude the public at all times
   B. admit the public at all times
   C. admit the public only if they are neat and well-dressed
   D. admit the public during specified hours

10. The key figure in any custodial safety program is the

    A. building custodian   B. cleaner
    C. operating engineer   D. commissioner

11. A supervisor should know the equipment used in his work well enough to

    A. make any repairs which might be needed
    B. know what parts to remove in case of breakdown
    C. anticipate any reasonable possibility of a breakdown
    D. know all the lubricants specified by the manufacturer

12. The PRIMARY responsibility of a building custodian is to

    A. make friends of all subordinates
    B. search for new methods of doing the work
    C. win the respect of his superior
    D. get the work done properly within a reasonable time

13. If the directions given by your superior are not clear, the BEST thing for you to do is to

A. ask to have the directions repeated and clarified
B. proceed to do the work taking a chance on doing the right thing
C. do nothing until some later time when you can find out exactly what is wanted
D. ask one of the other men in your crew what he would do under the circumstances

14. Of the following procedures concerning grievances of subordinate personnel, the custodian-engineer should maintain an attitude on

    A. paying little attention to little grievances
    B. being very alert to grievances and make adjustments in existing conditions to appease all personnel
    C. knowing the most frequent causes of grievances and strive to prevent them from arising
    D. maintaining firm discipline of a nature that *smooths out* all grievances

15. Of the following, the BEST course of action to take to settle a dispute or conflict between two employees is to

    A. insist that the two employees settle the case between themselves
    B. call in each one separately and, after hearing their cases presented, decide the issue
    C. bring both in for a conference at the same time and make the decision in their presence
    D. have both present their points of view and arguments in written memoranda and on this basis make your decision

16. If, as a custodian-engineer, you discover an error in your report submitted to the main office, you should

    A. do nothing, since it is possible that one error will have little effect on the total report
    B. wait until the error is discovered in the main office and then offer to work overtime to correct it
    C. go directly to the supervisor in the main office after working hours and ask him unofficially to correct the error
    D. notify the main office immediately so that the error can be corrected, if necessary

17. There are a considerable number of forms and reports to be submitted on schedule by the custodian-engineer. The ADVISABLE method of accomplishing this duty is to

    A. fill out the reports at odd times during the days when you have free time
    B. schedule a definite period of the work week for completing these forms and reports
    C. assign your foreman or cleaner to handle all these forms for you and to have them available on time
    D. classify or group the forms and reports and fill out only one of each group and refer the other forms or reports to the ones completed

18. A custodian-engineer can BEST evaluate the quality of work performed by custodial personnel by

    A. periodic inspection of the building's cleanliness
    B. studying the time records of personnel
    C. reviewing the building cleaning expenditures
    D. analyzing complaints of building occupants

19. Assume that you are the custodian-engineer and one of your employees wants to talk with you about a grievance. Of the following actions, the LEAST desirable action for you to take is to

    A. listen sympathetically
    B. conduct the discussion openly in the presence of the workforce
    C. try to get his point of view
    D. endeavor to obtain all the facts

20. Of the following factors, the one which is LEAST important in evaluating an employee and his work is his

    A. dependability
    B. quantity of work
    C. quality of work
    D. education and training

21. Supervision of a group of people engaged in building cleaning operations should NOT include supervision of

    A. time spent in cleaning operations
    B. utilization of official rest and lunch periods
    C. cleaning methods
    D. materials used for various cleaning jobs

22. Of the following methods, the BEST one to utilize in assigning custodial personnel to clean a multi-floor school building is to

    A. allow the cleaners to pick their rooms or area assignments out of a hat
    B. have the supervisor make specific room or area assignments to each cleaner separately
    C. rotate room and area assignments daily according to a chart posted on the bulletin board
    D. let a different member of the group make the room or area assignments each week

23. Assume that you are the custodian-engineer and that you have discovered a bottle of liquor in one of your employees' locker. The BEST course of action to take is to

    A. fire him immediately
    B. explain to him that liquor should not be brought into a school building and that a repetition may result in disciplinary action
    C. suspend him until the end of the week and take him back only on a probational basis
    D. assemble the staff and tell them they are all equally guilty for not having reported the matter to you

24. Of the following items, the one which is the LEAST important in the preparation of a report is that the report

    A. is brief, but to the point
    B. uses the prescribed form if there is one
    C. contains extra copies
    D. is accurate

25. In order to have building employees willing to follow standardized cleaning and mainte- 25._____
nance procedures, the supervisor must be prepared to
- A. work alongside the employees
- B. demonstrate the reasonableness of the procedures
- C. offer incentive pay for their utilization
- D. allow the employees the free use of the time saved by their adoption

KEY (CORRECT ANSWERS)

1.	A	11.	C
2.	D	12.	D
3.	B	13.	A
4.	B	14.	C
5.	D	15.	C
6.	C	16.	D
7.	D	17.	B
8.	D	18.	A
9.	D	19.	B
10.	A	20.	D

21.	B
22.	B
23.	B
24.	C
25.	B

PHILOSOPHY, PRINCIPLES, PRACTICES, AND TECHNICS OF SUPERVISION, ADMINISTRATION, MANAGEMENT, AND ORGANIZATION

TABLE OF CONTENTS

	Page
MEANING OF SUPERVISION	1
THE OLD AND THE NEW SUPERVISION	1
THE EIGHT (8) BASIC PRINCIPLES OF THE NEW SUPERVISION	1
I. Principle of Responsibility	1
II. Principle of Authority	2
III. Principle of Self-Growth	2
IV. Principle of Individual Worth	2
V. Principle of Creative Leadership	2
VI. Principle of Success and Failure	2
VII. Principle of Science	3
VIII. Principle of Cooperation	3
WHAT IS ADMINISTRATION?	3
I. Practices Commonly Classed as "Supervisory"	3
II. Practices Commonly Classed as "Administrative"	3
III. Practices Commonly Classed as Both "Supervisory" and "Administrative"	4
RESPONSIBILITIES OF THE SUPERVISOR	4
COMPETENCIES OF THE SUPERVISOR	4
THE PROFESSIONAL SUPERVISOR-EMPLOYEE RELATIONSHIP	4
MINI-TEXT IN SUPERVISION, ADMINISTRATION, MANAGEMENT, AND ORGANIZATION	5
I. Brief Highlights	5
A. Levels of Management	6
B. What the Supervisor Must Learn	6
C. A Definition of Supervision	6
D. Elements of the Team Concept	6
E. Principles of Organization	6
F. The Four Important Parts of Every Job	7
G. Principles of Delegation	7
H. Principles of Effective Communications	7
I. Principles of Work Improvement	7
J. Areas of Job Improvement	7
K. Seven Key Points in Making Improvements	8

	L.	Corrective Techniques for Job Improvement	8
	M.	A Planning Checklist	8
	N.	Five Characteristics of Good Directions	9
	O.	Types of Directions	9
	P.	Controls	9
	Q.	Orienting the New Employee	9
	R.	Checklist for Orienting New Employees	9
	S.	Principles of Learning	10
	T.	Causes of Poor Performance	10
	U.	Four Major Steps in On-the-Job Instructions	10
	V.	Employees Want Five Things	10
	W.	Some Don'ts in Regard to Praise	11
	X.	How to Gain Your Workers' Confidence	11
	Y.	Sources of Employee Problems	11
	Z.	The Supervisor's Key to Discipline	11
	AA.	Five Important Processes of Management	12
	BB.	When the Supervisor Fails to Plan	12
	CC.	Fourteen General Principles of Management	12
	DD.	Change	12
II.	Brief Topical Summaries		13
	A.	Who/What is the Supervisor?	13
	B.	The Sociology of Work	13
	C.	Principles and Practices of Supervision	14
	D.	Dynamic Leadership	14
	E.	Processes for Solving Problems	15
	F.	Training for Results	15
	G.	Health, Safety, and Accident Prevention	16
	H.	Equal Employment Opportunity	16
	I.	Improving Communications	16
	J.	Self-Development	17
	K.	Teaching and Training	17
		1. The Teaching Process	17
		a. Preparation	17
		b. Presentation	18
		c. Summary	18
		d. Application	18
		e. Evaluation	18
		2. Teaching Methods	18
		a. Lecture	18
		b. Discussion	18
		c. Demonstration	19
		d. Performance	19
		e. Which Method to Use	19

PHILOSOPHY, PRINCIPLES, PRACTICES, AND TECHNICS
OF
SUPERVISION, ADMINISTRATION, MANAGEMENT, AND ORGANIZATION

MEANING OF SUPERVISION

The extension of the democratic philosophy has been accompanied by an extension in the scope of supervision. Modern leaders and supervisors no longer think of supervision in the narrow sense of being confined chiefly to visiting employees, supplying materials, or rating the staff. They regard supervision as being intimately related to all the concerned agencies of society, they speak of the supervisor's function in terms of "growth," rather than the "improvement" of employees.

This modern concept of supervision may be defined as follows: Supervision is leadership and the development of leadership within groups which are cooperatively engaged in inspection, research, training, guidance, and evaluation.

THE OLD AND THE NEW SUPERVISION

TRADITIONAL
1. Inspection
2. Focused on the employee
3. Visitation
4. Random and haphazard
5. Imposed and authoritarian
6. One person usually

MODERN
1. Study and analysis
2. Focused on aims, materials, methods, supervisors, employees, environment
3. Demonstrations, intervisitation, workshops, directed reading, bulletins, etc.
4. Definitely organized and planned (scientific)
5. Cooperative and democratic
6. Many persons involved (creative)

THE EIGHT (8) BASIC PRINCIPLES OF THE NEW SUPERVISION

I. Principle of Responsibility
    Authority to act and responsibility for acting must be joined.
    A. If you give responsibility, give authority.
    B. Define employee duties clearly.
    C. Protect employees from criticism by others.
    D. Recognize the rights as well as obligations of employees.
    E. Achieve the aims of a democratic society insofar as it is possible within the area of your work.
    F. Establish a situation favorable to training and learning.
    G. Accept ultimate responsibility for everything done in your section, unit, office, division, department.
    H. Good administration and good supervision are inseparable.

II. Principle of Authority
The success of the supervisor is measured by the extent to which the power of authority is not used.
  A. Exercise simplicity and informality in supervision
  B. Use the simplest machinery of supervision
  C. If it is good for the organization as a whole, it is probably justified.
  D. Seldom be arbitrary or authoritative.
  E. Do not base your work on the power of position or of personality.
  F. Permit and encourage the free expression of opinions.

III. Principle of Self-Growth
The success of the supervisor is measured by the extent to which, and the speed with which, he is no longer needed.
  A. Base criticism on principles, not on specifics.
  B. Point out higher activities to employees.
  C. Train for self-thinking by employees to meet new situations.
  D. Stimulate initiative, self-reliance, and individual responsibility
  E. Concentrate on stimulating the growth of employees rather than on removing defects.

IV. Principle of Individual Worth
Respect for the individual is a paramount consideration in supervision.
  A. Be human and sympathetic in dealing with employees.
  B. Don't nag about things to be done.
  C. Recognize the individual differences among employees and seek opportunities to permit best expression of each personality.

V. Principle of Creative Leadership
The best supervision is that which is not apparent to the employee.
  A. Stimulate, don't drive employees to creative action.
  B. Emphasize doing good things.
  C. Encourage employees to do what they do best.
  D. Do not be too greatly concerned with details of subject or method.
  E. Do not be concerned exclusively with immediate problems and activities.
  F. Reveal higher activities and make them both desired and maximally possible.
  G. Determine procedures in the light of each situation but see that these are derived from a sound basic philosophy.
  H. Aid, inspire, and lead so as to liberate the creative spirit latent in all good employees.

VI. Principle of Success and Failure
There are no unsuccessful employees, only unsuccessful supervisors who have failed to give proper leadership.
  A. Adapt suggestions to the capacities, attitudes, and prejudices of employees.
  B. Be gradual, be progressive, be persistent.
  C. Help the employee find the general principle; have the employee apply his own problem to the general principle.
  D. Give adequate appreciation for good work and honest effort.
  E. Anticipate employee difficulties and help to prevent them.
  F. Encourage employees to do the desirable things they will do anyway.
  G. Judge your supervision by the results it secures.

VII. Principle of Science
Successful supervision is scientific, objective, and experimental. It is based on facts, not on prejudices.
   A. Be cumulative in results.
   B. Never divorce your suggestions from the goals of training.
   C. Don't be impatient of results.
   D. Keep all matters on a professional, not a personal, level.
   E. Do not be concerned exclusively with immediate problems and activities.
   F. Use objective means of determining achievement and rating where possible.

VIII. Principle of Cooperation
Supervision is a cooperative enterprise between supervisor and employee.
   A. Begin with conditions as they are.
   B. Ask opinions of all involved when formulating policies.
   C. Organization is as good as its weakest link.
   D. Let employees help to determine policies and department programs.
   E. Be approachable and accessible—physically and mentally.
   F. Develop pleasant social relationships.

WHAT IS ADMINISTRATION

Administration is concerned with providing the environment, the material facilities, and the operational procedures that will promote the maximum growth and development of supervisors and employees. (Organization is an aspect and a concomitant of administration.)

There is no sharp line of demarcation between supervision and administration; these functions are intimately interrelated and, often, overlapping. They are complementary activities.

I. Practices Commonly Classed as "Supervisory"
   A. Conducting employees' conferences
   B. Visiting sections, units, offices, divisions, departments
   C. Arranging for demonstrations
   D. Examining plans
   E. Suggesting professional reading
   F. Interpreting bulletins
   G. Recommending in-service training courses
   H. Encouraging experimentation
   I. Appraising employee morale
   J. Providing for intervisitation

II. Practices Commonly Classified as "Administrative"
   A. Management of the office
   B. Arrangement of schedules for extra duties
   C. Assignment of rooms or areas
   D. Distribution of supplies
   E. Keeping records and reports
   F. Care of audio-visual materials
   G. Keeping inventory records
   H. Checking record cards and books

    I.   Programming special activities
    J.   Checking on the attendance and punctuality of employees

III. Practices Commonly Classified as Both "Supervisory" and "Administrative"
    A. Program construction
    B. Testing or evaluating outcomes
    C. Personnel accounting
    D. Ordering instructional materials

RESPONSIBILITIES OF THE SUPERVISOR

A person employed in a supervisory capacity must constantly be able to improve his own efficiency and ability. He represent the employer to the employees and only continuous self-examination can make him a capable supervisor.

Leadership and training are the supervisor's responsibility. An efficient working unit is one in which the employees work with the supervisor. It is his job to bring out the best in his employees. He must always be relaxed, courteous, and calm in his association with his employees. Their feelings are important, and a harsh attitude does not develop the most efficient employees.

COMPETENCES OF THE SUPERVISOR

    I.   Complete knowledge of the duties and responsibilities of his position.
    II.   To be able to organize a job, plan ahead, and carry through.
    III.   To have self-confidence and initiative.
    IV.   To be able to handle the unexpected situation and make quick decisions.
    V.   To be able to properly train subordinates in the positions they are best suited for.
    VI.   To be able to keep good human relations among his subordinates.
    VII. To be able to keep good human relations between his subordinates and himself and to earn their respect and trust.

THE PROFESSIONAL SUPERVISOR-EMPLOYEE RELATIONSHIP

There are two kinds of efficiency: one kind is only apparent and is produced in organizations through the exercise of mere discipline; this is but a simulation of the second, or true, efficiency which springs from spontaneous cooperation. If you are a manager, no matter how great or small your responsibility, it is your job, in the final analysis, to create and develop this involuntary cooperation among the people whom you supervise. For, no matter how powerful a combination of money, machines, and materials a company may have, this is a dead and sterile thing without a team of willing, thinking, and articulate people to guide it.

The following 21 points are presented as indicative of the exemplary basic relationship that should exist between supervisor and employee:

1. Each person wants to be liked and respected by his fellow employee and wants to be treated with consideration and respect by his superior.
2. The most competent employee will make an error. However, in a unit where good relations exist between the supervisor and his employees, tenseness and fear do not exist. Thus, errors are not hidden or covered up, and the efficiency of a unit is not impaired.

3. Subordinates resent rules, regulations, or orders that are unreasonable or unexplained.
4. Subordinates are quick to resent unfairness, harshness, injustices, and favoritism.
5. An employee will accept responsibility if he knows that he will be complimented for a job well done, and not too harshly chastised for failure; that his supervisor will check the cause of the failure, and, if it was the supervisor's fault, he will assume the blame therefore. If it was the employee's fault, his supervisor will explain the correct method or means of handling the responsibility.
6. An employee wants to receive credit for a suggestion he has made, that is used. If a suggestion cannot be used, the employee is entitled to an explanation. The supervisor should not say "no" and close the subject.
7. Fear and worry slow up a worker's ability. Poor working environment can impair his physical and mental health. A good supervisor avoids forceful methods, threats, and arguments to get a job done.
8. A forceful supervisor is able to train his employees individually and as a team, and is able to motivate them in the proper channels.
9. A mature supervisor is able to properly evaluate his subordinates and to keep them happy and satisfied.
10. A sensitive supervisor will never patronize his subordinates.
11. A worthy supervisor will respect his employees' confidences.
12. Definite and clear-cut responsibilities should be assigned to each executive.
13. Responsibility should always be coupled with corresponding authority.
14. No change should be made in the scope or responsibilities of a position without a definite understanding to that effect on the part of all persons concerned.
15. No executive or employee, occupying a single position in the organization, should be subject to definite orders from more than one source.
16. Orders should never be given to subordinates over the head of a responsible executive. Rather than do this, the officer in question should be supplanted.
17. Criticisms of subordinates should, whoever possible, be made privately, and in no case should a subordinate be criticized in the presence of executives or employees of equal or lower rank.
18. No dispute or difference between executives or employees as to authority or responsibilities should be considered too trivial for prompt and careful adjudication.
19. Promotions, wage changes, and disciplinary action should always be approved by the executive immediately superior to the one directly responsible.
20. No executive or employee should ever be required, or expected, to be at the same time an assistant to, and critic of, another.
21. Any executive whose work is subject to regular inspection should, wherever practicable, be given the assistance and facilities necessary to enable him to maintain an independent check of the quality of his work.

MINI-TEXT IN SUPERVISION, ADMINISTRATION, MANAGEMENT, AND ORGANIZATION

I. Brief Highlights

Listed concisely and sequentially are major headings and important data in the field for quick recall and review.

A. Levels of Management
Any organization of some size has several levels of management. In terms of a ladder, the levels are:

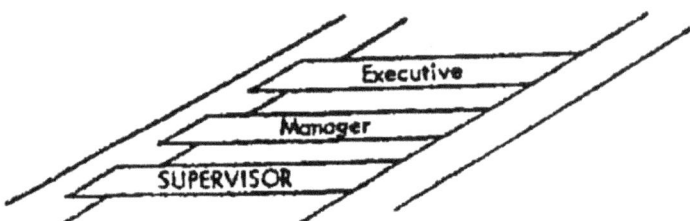

The first level is very important because it is the beginning point of management leadership.

B. What the Supervisor Must Learn
A supervisor must learn to:
1. Deal with people and their differences
2. Get the job done through people
3. Recognize the problems when they exist
4. Overcome obstacles to good performance
5. Evaluate the performance of people
6. Check his own performance in terms of accomplishment

C. A Definition of Supervisor
The term supervisor means any individual having authority, in the interests of the employer, to hire, transfer, suspend, lay-off, recall, promote, discharge, assign, reward, or discipline other employees or responsibility to direct them, or to adjust their grievances, or effectively to recommend such action, if, in connection with the foregoing, exercise of such authority is not of a merely routine or clerical nature but requires the use of independent judgment.

D. Elements of the Team Concept
What is involved in teamwork? The component parts are:
1. Members
2. A leader
3. Goals
4. Plans
5. Cooperation
6. Spirit

E. Principles of Organization
1. A team member must know what his job is.
2. Be sure that the nature and scope of a job are understood.
3. Authority and responsibility should be carefully spelled out.
4. A supervisor should be permitted to make the maximum number of decisions affecting his employees.
5. Employees should report to only one supervisor.
6. A supervisor should direct only as many employees as he can handle effectively.
7. An organization plan should be flexible.

8. Inspection and performance of work should be separate.
9. Organizational problems should receive immediate attention.
10. Assign work in line with ability and experience.

F. The Four Important Parts of Every Job
1. Inherent in every job is the *accountability* for results.
2. A second set of factors in every job is *responsibilities*.
3. Along with duties and responsibilities one must have the *authority* to act within certain limits without obtaining permission to proceed.
4. No job exists in a vacuum. The supervisor is surrounded by key *relationships*.

G. Principles of Delegation
Where work is delegated for the first time, the supervisor should think in terms of these questions:
1. Who is best qualified to do this?
2. Can an employee improve his abilities by doing this?
3. How long should an employee spend on this?
4. Are there any special problems for which he will need guidance?
5. How broad a delegation can I make?

H. Principles of Effective Communications
1. Determine the media.
2. To whom directed?
3. Identification and source authority.
4. Is communication understood?

I. Principles of Work Improvement
1. Most people usually do only the work which is assigned to them.
2. Workers are likely to fit assigned work into the time available to perform it.
3. A good workload usually stimulates output.
4. People usually do their best work when they know that results will be reviewed or inspected.
5. Employees usually feel that someone else is responsible for conditions of work, workplace layout, job methods, type of tools/equipment, and other such factors.
6. Employees are usually defensive about their job security.
7. Employees have natural resistance to change.
8. Employees can support or destroy a supervisor.
9. A supervisor usually earns the respect of his people through his personal example of diligence and efficiency.

J. Areas of Job Improvement
The areas of job improvement are quite numerous, but the most common ones which a supervisor can identify and utilize are:
1. Departmental layout
2. Flow of work
3. Workplace layout
4. Utilization of manpower
5. Work methods
6. Materials handling

7. Utilization
8. Motion economy

K. Seven Key Points in Making Improvements
1. Select the job to be improved
2. Study how it is being done now
3. Question the present method
4. Determine actions to be taken
5. Chart proposed method
6. Get approval and apply
7. Solicit worker participation

L. Corrective Techniques of Job Improvement
Specific Problems
1. Size of workload
2. Inability to meet schedules
3. Strain and fatigue
4. Improper use of men and skills
5. Waste, poor quality, unsafe conditions
6. Bottleneck conditions that hinder output
7. Poor utilization of equipment and machine
8. Efficiency and productivity of labor

General Improvement
1. Departmental layout
2. Flow of work
3. Work plan layout
4. Utilization of manpower
5. Work methods
6. Materials handling
7. Utilization of equipment
8. Motion economy

Corrective Techniques
1. Study with scale model
2. Flow chart study
3. Motion analysis
4. Comparison of units produced to standard allowance
5. Methods analysis
6. Flow chart and equipment study
7. Down time vs. running time
8. Motion analysis

M. A Planning Checklist
1. Objectives
2. Controls
3. Delegations
4. Communications
5. Resources
6. Manpower

7. Equipment
8. Supplies and materials
9. Utilization of time
10. Safety
11. Money
12. Work
13. Timing of improvements

N. Five Characteristics of Good Directions
In order to get results, directions must be:
1. Possible of accomplishment
2. Agreeable with worker interests
3. Related to mission
4. Planned and complete
5. Unmistakably clear

O. Types of Directions
1. Demands or direct orders
2. Requests
3. Suggestion or implication
4. volunteering

P. Controls
A typical listing of the overall areas in which the supervisor should establish controls might be:
1. Manpower
2. Materials
3. Quality of work
4. Quantity of work
5. Time
6. Space
7. Money
8. Methods

Q. Orienting the New Employee
1. Prepare for him
2. Welcome the new employee
3. Orientation for the job
4. Follow-up

R. Checklist for Orienting New Employees   Yes   No
1. Do you appreciate the feelings of new employees
   when they first report for work?   ___   ___
2. Are you aware of the fact that the new employee must
   make a big adjustment to his job?   ___   ___
3. Have you given him good reasons for liking the job and
   the organization?   ___   ___
4. Have you prepared for his first day on the job? ___   ___
5. Did you welcome him cordially and make him feel needed? ___ ___

			Yes	No
6.	Did you establish rapport with him so that he feels free to talk and discuss matters with you?		___	___
7.	Did you explain his job to him and his relationship to you?		___	___
8.	Does he know that his work will be evaluated periodically on a basis that is fair and objective?		___	___
9.	Did you introduce him to his fellow workers in such a way that they are likely to accept him?		___	___
10.	Does he know what employee benefits he will receive?		___	___
11.	Does he understand the importance of being on the job and what to do if he must leave his duty station?		___	___
12.	Has he been impressed with the importance of accident prevention and safe practice?		___	___
13.	Does he generally know his way around the department?		___	___
14.	Is he under the guidance of a sponsor who will teach the right way of doing things?		___	___
15.	Do you plan to follow-up so that he will continue to adjust successfully to his job?		___	___

S. Principles of Learning
1. Motivation
2. Demonstration or explanation
3. Practice

T. Causes of Poor Performance
1. Improper training for job
2. Wrong tools
3. Inadequate directions
4. Lack of supervisory follow-up
5. Poor communications
6. Lack of standards of performance
7. Wrong work habits
8. Low morale
9. Other

U. Four Major Steps in On-The-Job Instruction
1. Prepare the worker
2. Present the operation
3. Tryout performance
4. Follow-up

V. Employees Want Five Things
1. Security
2. Opportunity
3. Recognition
4. Inclusion
5. Expression

W. Some Don'ts in Regard to Praise
1. Don't praise a person for something he hasn't done.
2. Don't praise a person unless you can be sincere.
3. Don't be sparing in praise just because your superior withholds it from you.
4. Don't let too much time elapse between good performance and recognition of it

X. How to Gain Your Workers' Confidence
Methods of developing confidence include such things as:
1. Knowing the interests, habits, hobbies of employees
2. Admitting your own inadequacies
3. Sharing and telling of confidence in others
4. Supporting people when they are in trouble
5. Delegating matters that can be well handled
6. Being frank and straightforward about problems and working conditions
7. Encouraging others to bring their problems to you
8. Taking action on problems which impede worker progress

Y. Sources of Employee Problems
On-the-job causes might be such things as:
1. A feeling that favoritism is exercised in assignments
2. Assignment of overtime
3. An undue amount of supervision
4. Changing methods or systems
5. Stealing of ideas or trade secrets
6. Lack of interest in job
7. Threat of reduction in force
8. Ignorance or lack of communications
9. Poor equipment
10. Lack of knowing how supervisor feels toward employee
11. Shift assignments

Off-the-job problems might have to do with:
1. Health
2. Finances
3. Housing
4. Family

Z. The Supervisor's Key to Discipline
There are several key points about discipline which the supervisor should keep in mind:
1. Job discipline is one of the disciplines of life and is directed by the supervisor.
2. It is more important to correct an employee fault than to fix blame for it.
3. Employee performance is affected by problems both on the job and off.
4. Sudden or abrupt changes in behavior can be indications of important employee problems.
5. Problems should be dealt with as soon as possible after they are identified.
6. The attitude of the supervisor may have more to do with solving problems than the techniques of problem solving.
7. Correction of employee behavior should be resorted to only after the supervisor is sure that training or counseling will not be helpful.

8. Be sure to document your disciplinary actions.
9. Make sure that you are disciplining on the basis of facts rather than personal feelings.
10. Take each disciplinary step in order, being careful not to make snap judgments, or decisions based on impatience.

AA. Five Important Processes of Management
1. Planning
2. Organizing
3. Scheduling
4. Controlling
5. Motivating

BB. When the Supervisor Fails to Plan
1. Supervisor creates impression of not knowing his job
2. May lead to excessive overtime
3. Job runs itself—supervisor lacks control
4. Deadlines and appointments missed
5. Parts of the work go undone
6. Work interrupted by emergencies
7. Sets a bad example
8. Uneven workload creates peaks and valleys
9. Too much time on minor details at expense of more important tasks

CC. Fourteen General Principles of Management
1. Division of work
2. Authority and responsibility
3. Discipline
4. Unity of command
5. Unity of direction
6. Subordination of individual interest to general interest
7. Remuneration of personnel
8. Centralization
9. Scalar chain
10. Order
11. Equity
12. Stability of tenure of personnel
13. Initiative
14. Esprit de corps

DD. Change

Bringing about change is perhaps attempted more often, and yet less well understood, than anything else the supervisor does. How do people generally react to change? (People tend to resist change that is imposed upon them by other individuals or circumstances.

Change is characteristic of every situation. It is a part of every real endeavor where the efforts of people are concerned.

1. Why do people resist change?
   People may resist change because of:
   a. Fear of the unknown
   b. Implied criticism
   c. Unpleasant experiences in the past
   d. Fear of loss of status
   e. Threat to the ego
   f. Fear of loss of economic stability

2. How can we best overcome the resistance to change?
   In initiating change, take these steps:
   a. Get ready to sell
   b. Identify sources of help
   c. Anticipate objections
   d. Sell benefits
   e. Listen in depth
   f. Follow up

II. Brief Topical Summaries

   A. Who/What is the Supervisor?
      1. The supervisor is often called the "highest level employee and the lowest level manager."
      2. A supervisor is a member of both management and the work group. He acts as a bridge between the two.
      3. Most problems in supervision are in the area of human relations, or people problems.
      4. Employees expect: Respect, opportunity to learn and to advance, and a sense of belonging, and so forth.
      5. Supervisors are responsible for directing people and organizing work. Planning is of paramount importance.
      6. A position description is a set of duties and responsibilities inherent to a given position.
      7. It is important to keep the position description up-to-date and to provide each employee with his own copy.

   B. The Sociology of Work
      1. People are alike in many ways; however, each individual is unique.
      2. The supervisor is challenged in getting to know employee differences. Acquiring skills in evaluating individuals is an asset.
      3. Maintaining meaningful working relationships in the organization is of great importance.
      4. The supervisor has an obligation to help individuals to develop to their fullest potential.
      5. Job rotation on a planned basis helps to build versatility and to maintain interest and enthusiasm in work groups.
      6. Cross training (job rotation) provides backup skills.

7. The supervisor can help reduce tension by maintaining a sense of humor, providing guidance to employees, and by making reasonable and timely decisions. Employees respond favorably to working under reasonably predictable circumstances.
8. Change is characteristic of all managerial behavior. The supervisor must adjust to changes in procedures, new methods, technological changes, and to a number of new and sometimes challenging situations.
9. To overcome the natural tendency for people to resist change, the supervisor should become more skillful in initiating change.

C. Principles and Practices of Supervision
1. Employees should be required to answer to only one superior.
2. A supervisor can effectively direct only a limited number of employees, depending upon the complexity, variety, and proximity of the jobs involved.
3. The organizational chart presents the organization in graphic form. It reflects lines of authority and responsibility as well as interrelationships of units within the organization.
4. Distribution of work can be improved through an analysis using the "Work Distribution Chart."
5. The "Work Distribution Chart" reflects the division of work within a unit in understandable form.
6. When related tasks are given to an employee, he has a better chance of increasing his skills through training.
7. The individual who is given the responsibility for tasks must also be given the appropriate authority to insure adequate results.
8. The supervisor should delegate repetitive, routine work. Preparation of recurring reports, maintaining leave and attendance records are some examples.
9. Good discipline is essential to good task performance. Discipline is reflected in the actions of employees on the job in the absence of supervision.
10. Disciplinary action may have to be taken when the positive aspects of discipline have failed. Reprimand, warning, and suspension are examples of disciplinary action.
11. If a situation calls for a reprimand, be sure it is deserved and remember it is to be done in private.

D. Dynamic Leadership
1. A style is a personal method or manner of exerting influence.
2. Authoritarian leaders often see themselves as the source of power and authority.
3. The democratic leader often perceives the group as the source of authority and power.
4. Supervisors tend to do better when using the pattern of leadership that is most natural for them.
5. Social scientists suggest that the effective supervisor use the leadership style that best fits the problem or circumstances involved.
6. All four styles—telling, selling, consulting, joining—have their place. Using one does not preclude using the other at another time.

7. The theory X point of view assumes that the average person dislikes work, will avoid it whenever possible, and must be coerced to achieve organizational objectives.
8. The theory Y point of view assumes that the average person considers work to be a natural as play, and, when the individual is committed, he requires little supervision or direction to accomplish desired objectives.
9. The leader's basic assumptions concerning human behavior and human nature affect his actions, decisions, and other managerial practices.
10. Dissatisfaction among employees is often present, but difficult to isolate. The supervisor should seek to weaken dissatisfaction by keeping promises, being sincere and considerate, keeping employees informed, and so forth.
11. Constructive suggestions should be encouraged during the natural progress of the work.

E. Processes for Solving Problems
1. People find their daily tasks more meaningful and satisfying when they can improve them.
2. The causes of problems, or the key factors, are often hidden in the background. Ability to solve problems often involves the ability to isolate them from their backgrounds. There is some substance to the cliché that some persons "can't see the forest for the trees."
3. New procedures are often developed from old ones. Problems should be broken down into manageable parts. New ideas can be adapted from old one.
4. People think differently in problem-solving situations. Using a logical, patterned approach is often useful. One approach found to be useful includes these steps:
   a. Define the problem
   b. Establish objectives
   c. Get the facts
   d. Weigh and decide
   e. Take action
   f. Evaluate action

F. Training for Results
1. Participants respond best when they feel training is important to them.
2. The supervisor has responsibility for the training and development of those who report to him.
3. When training is delegated to others, great care must be exercised to insure the trainer has knowledge, aptitude, and interest for his work as a trainer.
4. Training (learning) of some type goes on continually. The most successful supervisor makes certain the learning contributes in a productive manner to operational goals.
5. New employees are particularly susceptible to training. Older employees facing new job situations require specific training, as well as having need for development and growth opportunities.
6. Training needs require continuous monitoring.
7. The training officer of an agency is a professional with a responsibility to assist supervisors in solving training problems.

8. Many of the self-development steps important to the supervisor's own growth are equally important to the development of peers and subordinates. Knowledge of these is important when the supervisor consults with others on development and growth opportunities.

G. Health, Safety, and Accident Prevention
1. Management-minded supervisors take appropriate measures to assist employees in maintaining health and in assuring safe practices in the work environment.
2. Effective safety training and practices help to avoid injury and accidents.
3. Safety should be a management goal. All infractions of safety which are observed should be corrected without exception.
4. Employees' safety attitude, training and instruction, provision of safe tools and equipment, supervision, and leadership are considered highly important factors which contribute to safety and which can be influenced directly by supervisors.
5. When accidents do occur, they should be investigated promptly for very important reasons, including the fact that information which is gained can be used to prevent accidents in the future.

H. Equal Employment Opportunity
1. The supervisor should endeavor to treat all employees fairly, without regard to religion, race, sex, or national origin.
2. Groups tend to reflect the attitude of the leader. Prejudice can be detected even in very subtle form. Supervisors must strive to create a feeling of mutual respect and confidence in every employee.
3. Complete utilization of all human resources is a national goal. Equitable consideration should be accorded women in the work force, minority-group members, the physically and mentally handicapped, and the older employee. The important question is: "Who can do the job?"
4. Training opportunities, recognition for performance, overtime assignments, promotional opportunities, and all other personnel actions are to be handled on an equitable basis.

I. Improving Communications
1. Communications is achieving understanding between the sender and the receiver of a message. It also means sharing information—the creation of understanding.
2. Communication is basic to all human activity. Words are means of conveying meanings; however, real meanings are in people.
3. There are very practical differences in the effectiveness of one-way, impersonal, and two-way communications. Words spoken face-to-face are better understood. Telephone conversations are effective, but lack the rapport of person-to-person exchanges. The whole person communicates.
4. Cooperation and communication in an organization go hand in hand. When there is a mutual respect between people, spelling out rules and procedures for communicating is unnecessary.
5. There are several barriers to effective communications. These include failure to listen with respect and understanding, lack of skill in feedback, and misinterpreting the meanings of words used by the speaker. It is also common

practice to listen to what we want to hear, and tune out things we do not want to hear.
6. Communication is management's chief problem. The supervisor should accept the challenge to communicate more effectively and to improve interagency and intra-agency communications.
7. The supervisor may often plan for and conduct meetings. The planning phase is critical and may determine the success or the failure of a meeting.
8. Speaking before groups usually requires extra effort. Stage fright may never disappear completely, but it can be controlled.

J. Self-Development
1. Every employee is responsible for his own self-development.
2. Toastmaster and toastmistress clubs offer opportunities to improve skills in oral communications.
3. Planning for one's own self-development is of vital importance. Supervisors know their own strengths and limitations better than anyone else.
4. Many opportunities are open to aid the supervisor in his developmental efforts, including job assignments; training opportunities, both governmental and non-governmental—to include universities and professional conferences and seminars.
5. Programmed instruction offers a means of studying at one's own rate.
6. Where difficulties may arise from a supervisor's being away from his work for training, he may participate in televised home study or correspondence courses to meet his self-development needs.

K. Teaching and Training
1. The Teaching Process
Teaching is encouraging and guiding the learning activities of students toward established goals. In most cases this process consists of five steps: preparation, presentation, summarization, evaluation, and application.

    a. Preparation
Preparation is two-fold in nature; that of the supervisor and the employee. Preparation by the supervisor is absolutely essential to success. He must know what, when, where, how, and whom he will teach. Some of the factors that should be considered are:
1) The objectives
2) The materials needed
3) The methods to be used
4) Employee participation
5) Employee interest
6) Training aids
7) Evaluation
8) Summarization

Employee preparation consists in preparing the employee to receive the material. Probably the most important single factor in the preparation of the employee is arousing and maintaining his interest. He must know the objectives of the training, why he is there, how the material can be used, and its importance to him.

b. Presentation
In presentation, have a carefully designed plan and follow it. The plan should be accurate and complete, yet flexible enough to meet situations as they arise. The method of presentation will be determined by the particular situation and objectives.

c. Summary
A summary should be made at the end of every training unit and program. In addition, there may be internal summaries depending on the nature of the material being taught. The important thing is that the trainee must always be able to understand how each part of the new material relates to the whole.

d. Application
The supervisor must arrange work so the employee will be given a chance to apply new knowledge or skills while the material is still clear in his mind and interest is high. The trainee does not really know whether he has learned the material until he has been given a chance to apply it. If the material is not applied, it loses most of its value.

e. Evaluation
The purpose of all training is to promote learning. To determine whether the training has been a success or failure, the supervisor must evaluate this learning.
In the broadest sense, evaluation includes all the devices, methods, skills, and techniques used by the supervisor to keep himself and the employees informed as to their progress toward the objectives they are pursuing. The extent to which the employee has mastered the knowledge, skills, and abilities, or changed his attitudes, as determined by the program objectives, is the extent to which instruction has succeeded or failed.
Evaluation should not be confined to the end of the lesson, day, or program but should be used continuously. We shall note later the way this relates to the rest of the teaching process.

2. Teaching Methods
A teaching method is a pattern of identifiable student and instructor activity used in presenting training material.
All supervisors are faced with the problem of deciding which method should be used at a given time.

a. Lecture
The lecture is direct oral presentation of material by the supervisor. The present trend is to place less emphasis on the trainer's activity and more on that of the trainee.

b. Discussion
Teaching by discussion or conference involves using questions and other techniques to arouse interest and focus attention upon certain areas, and by doing so creating a learning situation. This can be one of the most

valuable methods because it gives the employees an opportunity to express their ideas and pool their knowledge.

    c. Demonstration
The demonstration is used to teach how something works or how to do something. It can be used to show a principle or what the results of a series of actions will be. A well-staged demonstration is particularly effective because it shows proper methods of performance in a realistic manner.

    d. Performance
Performance is one of the most fundamental of all learning techniques or teaching methods. The trainee may be able to tell how a specific operation should be performed but he cannot be sure he knows how to perform the operation until he has done so.
As with all methods, there are certain advantages and disadvantages to each method.

    e. Which Method to Use
Moreover, there are other methods and techniques of teaching. It is difficult to use any method without other methods entering into it. In any learning situation, a combination of methods is usually more effective than any one method alone.

Finally, evaluation must be integrated into the other aspects of the teaching-learning process.

It must be used in the motivation of the trainees; it must be used to assist in developing understanding during the training; and it must be related to employee application of the results of training.

This is distinctly the role of the supervisor.

USE AND CARE OF EQUIPMENT, MATERIALS, AND SUPPLIES

TABLE OF CONTENTS

		Page
I.	GENERAL POINTS TO BE OBSERVED	1
II.	USE AND CARE OF NON-AUTOMATIC/MANUAL EQUIPMENT	3
III.	USE AND CARE OF AUTOMATIC EQUIPMENT	8
IV.	HELPFUL SERVICE HINTS FOR WET AND DRY VACUUM	11
V.	HELPFUL SERVICE HINTS FOR FLOOR MACHINES	13
VI.	HELPFUL SERVICE HINTS FOR AUTOMATIC SCRUBBERS	14

USE AND CARE OF EQUIPMENT, MATERIALS, AND SUPPLIES

I. GENERAL POINTS TO BE OBSERVED

The institution has invested a large amount of money in expensive modern equipment, materials, and supplies in order to help fulfill the housekeeping goals. Therefore, it is the responsibility of each employee to keep the equipment in good working condition and use materials and supplies economically.

Storing of equipment is part of the housekeeping aid's job in caring for equipment. Some institutions have storage areas or utility rooms located in each department or on each floor. Others have central equipment rooms near the housekeeper's office. These areas are equipped with hooks, racks, shelves, sinks, and floor drains for the cleaning and storing of equipment, materials, and supplies.

The storage area must be maintained daily and every item must have a place.

Care of equipment, materials, and supplies are divided into two groups: care of non-automatic/manual equipment, and care of power-operated (electric or battery) equipment. However, there are several general points to be observed on the care and upkeep of all equipment, materials, and supplies.

1. Follow manufacturer's instructions for operation and maintenance.

2. Provide a preventive maintenance program (routine and systematic inspections and repairs).

3. Replace equipment, materials, or supplies promptly when faulty or ineffective.

4. Keep equipment clean at all times.

5. Use materials and supplies economically.

6. Provide adequate and proper storage area for equipment, materials, and supplies.

7. Use each piece of equipment only for its intended purpose.

8. Report faulty, damaged, or ineffective materials or equipment to the supervisor.

PURPOSE: To maintain equipment in good working condition; to insure faster, easier, and more efficient performance; to control bacteria and for appearance.

EQUIPMENT:
    Germicidal detergent
    Cloths or sponges
    Buckets (two)
    Gloves

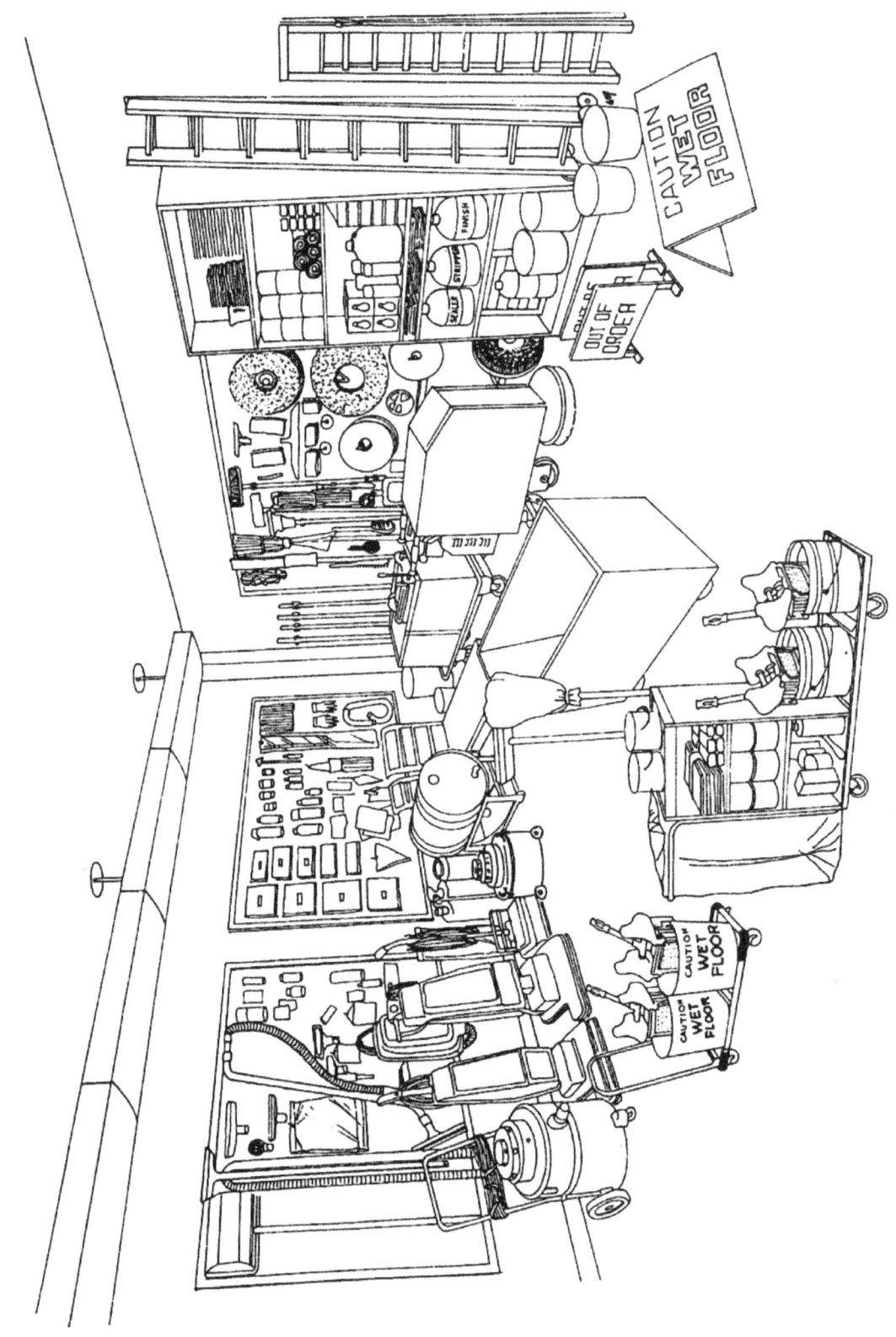

SAFETY PRECAUTIONS:

1. Never pour used sealer or finish back into clean solution containers.

2. Brushes should never be stored on the bristles or left on machines.

3. Do not use more of an item than is necessary to efficiently perform the task.

4. Make sure pressure is released from wall washing tanks before cleaning.

5. All equipment must be cleaned at the end of the day and returned to designated storage area.

II. USE AND CARE OF NON-AUTOMATIC/MANUAL EQUIPMENT

Included in this type of equipment are items used in housekeeping duties that are entirely moved or operated by hand. This includes everything from brushes to wall washing pressure tanks.

EQUIPMENT:
- Utility carts
- Brushes of all types:
    a. Counter
    b. Sweeping
    c. Toilet
    d. Deck and other scrub brushes
    e. Radiator
    f. Scrub and polish
    g. Pot
    h. Nylon hand brush
    i. Coving or baseboard
- Dustpans
- Screens, sifters, and slit spoons
- Caution signs
- Squeegees
- Buckets (small and large)
- Dollies
- Wringers
- Mopheads
- Nylon pads
- Sweeping floor tools
- Extension handles
- Trash carts
- Wall washing pressure tanks
- Ladders
- Gloves
- Sealers
- Strippers (bulk and portioned)
- Finishes (bulk and portioned)
- Germicidal detergents (bulk and portioned)
- Polishes (furniture, stainless steel)
- Treated cloths
- Dust cloths
- Soaps
- Plastic liners
- Carpet sweepers
- Putty knives
- Hose (water)
- Measuring cups
- Mopping tanks
- Spray units
- Toilet tissue
- Paper towels
- Bottles (plastic)
- Trash containers
- Corn brooms

PROCEDURE

Utility Carts

1. Wipe off all shelves with germicidal cloth at the end of the day. Dry.
2. Place plastic liner on top shelf to keep from rusting.
3. Use it daily in performing duties as assigned.
4. Keep shelves neatly stocked with all supplies and equipment.

Brushes

1. Clean at the end of the day.
2. Comb with a stiff fiber brush or comb and wash under running water. Shake out excess water.
3. Store by hanging on rack, free from touching any surface or store on block/wood part of the brush.
4. Do not use until bristles are dry.
5. For maximum wear and effectiveness, brushes with removable handles should be rotated at least once a week.
6. Always hang broom up. Never stand on the straws.

Bottles (Plastic Spray Bottle)

1. Clean exterior with paper towel dipped in germicidal solution. Dry.
2. Return to utility cart.
3. A trigger type must be taken apart regularly and washed and rinsed thoroughly.

Carpet Sweepers

1. Empty into plastic liner after each use. Place liner in trash collection container.
2. Remove strings and debris from brush and wheel.
3. Damp wipe the sweeper.

Caution Signs (Wet Floor, Out of Order)

1. Damp wipe and dry after each use.
2. Periodically, thoroughly wash, rinse, and dry.

Cloths (Treated and Cleaning)

1. Treated
   a. Use all surfaces of the woven treated paper before discarding.
   b. Treat own cloths by spraying lightly with solution and allow to stand overnight in covered container. May be discarded or laundered.
2. Cleaning:
   a. Rinse frequently during use.
   b. At the end of the day or at the end of the bathroom cleaning procedure, place cleaning cloths in plastic liner, then put into a regular laundry bag for laundering.
   c. Never leave cloths lying around.

Dustpans

1. Clean at the end of the day. Wash with germicidal solution.
2. Rinse and dry.
3. Hang on hook on cart so that it will not become bent or damaged.

Extension Handles

1. Use as an aid for high dusting.
2. Wipe off daily.

Floor Sweeping Tools

1. Use a disposable cloth.
2. Use all surfaces possible.
3. Damp wipe handle and foot frame daily.
4. Wash tool once a week with germicidal detergent.
5. Hang up on utility cart when not in use.

Germicidal Detergents and Strippers

1. Used in the cleaning operation to remove soil.
2. Do not overuse—will destroy flooring surfaces.
3. Use recommended amount only.
4. Read label before using.

Gloves

1. Wash outside of gloves under running water (while on hand) at the end of the day.
2. Remove and wash inside. Wipe dry.
3. Hang across a smooth surface to dry.

Hose (With Cut-off Nozzle)

1. Rinse off rubber or plastic hose.
2. Roll in a three-foot circle to prevent kinking. Drain water while rolling.
3. Hang hose on a rack or peg in storage area.

Knives (Putty—Short and Long)

1. Wipe handle and blade with germicidal solution at end of day. Dry.
2. Return to cart.

Ladders (Safety and Platform)

1. Wipe off after each use with germicidal solution.
2. Rinse and dry.
3. Return to designated storage area.

Measuring Cups

1. Rinse immediately after use.
2. Dry.
3. Store so that it will not be damaged.

Mops—Dust

1. Do not use to mop up spills.
2. Remove loose soil from mop frequently, by vacuum if possible.
3. Remove mophead at end of day, place in plastic bag and take to designated storage area for laundering.

Mops—Wet

1. Cut off loose and uneven yarn strands.
2. Never twist or squeeze mop extra hard; such action will break fibers and destroy the mophead.
3. Remove mophead at the end of bathroom cleaning and at the end of the day.
4. Place in plastic bag and into laundry bag and take to designated storage area for laundering.

Mopping Tanks, Buckets, Wringers, and Dollies

1. Remove any loose mophead yarn, string, or foreign matter.
2. Wash, rinse, and dry daily. Invert small and medium size buckets to dry.
3. Keep the equipment in good repair. Report any defects to supervisor.
4. When necessary, add a few drops of oil to casters.
5. Avoid hitting the mopping unit against other objects and walls.
6. Replace bumper strip when needed.
7. Do not allow a cleaning solution to remain in the bucket when the bucket is not in use.

Small Buckets or Pails

1. Empty contents.
2. Wash, rinse, and dry.
3. Turn upside down to dry.

Polishes

1. Used on furniture, stainless steel, wood, and metal.
2. Use only the recommended amount.
3. It is very annoying to get polish on one's clothes, so thoroughly rub the surface to remove excess polish.

Paper Towels and Toilet Tissue

1. Replacement supplies.
2. Always place in containers, not in window sills or on top of cabinets.

Screens, Sifters/Slit Spoons

1. Wash and shake off excess water.
2. Dry. Handle so as not to bend screen.
3. Place on hook on utility cart or other designated storage area.

Nylon Pads

1. Wash pads under running water. Rinse.
2. Hang or store on flat surface until dry.

Plastic Liners

1. Used to line trash containers.
2. Must be replaced daily.
3. Do not use for any other purpose than intended.

Sealers, Finishers

1. Items used to protect flooring.
2. These items are very expensive.
3. Use liners in buckets when using sealer and finish.
4. Never pour solution on floor.
5. Wipe up spills or drips immediately.
6. Never waste the product. Pour just enough on mophead in bucket to wet mophead, which should eliminate any material being left over.
7. In case there is a small amount left over, discard it. Do not pour into clean solution; solution will sour.
8. Mopheads should be placed in plastic liner/bag for laundering.
9. Wash, rinse, and dry buckets, wringers, dolly, mops, and mop handles used in these operations.

Soaps

1. Used for hand washing and bathing.
2. Must rinse before using.
3. Not used for cleaning inanimate surfaces.

Sponges

1. Place in germicidal solution. Wash thoroughly. Squeeze out excess water.
2. Rinse. Squeeze out excess water.
3. Place on flat surface to dry. Do not hang on nails.

Squeegees (Small or Large)

1. Wash squeegee blades in germicidal solution.
2. Rinse. Drain off excess water.
3. Wipe dry and return to utility cart or storage area.
4. Do not store with squeegee blades down.

Spray Units

1. Used for spray buffing and dry stripping.
2. Wipe off with germicidal solution.
3. Rinse spray nozzles.
4. Do not let material harden on nozzle.

Trash Containers

1. Used to receive or hold waste.
2. Handle containers so as not to scratch, puncture, or bend them.
3. Wipe trash container inside and out daily. Replace liner.
4. Once a month, collect trash containers, take to utility room, and thoroughly wash, rinse, and dry or steam clean.

Trash Carts

1. Used for general collection of trash.
2. Take to utility room. Wash inside and outside thoroughly. Let drain.
3. Rinse and let drain.
4. Wipe dry.

Wall Washing Machines/Pressure Tanks

1. Empty at the end of the operation.
2. Rinse tubing and inside of tanks.
3. Wipe off outside with germicidal detergent. Dry.
4. Store in designated storage area.

III. USE AND CARE OF AUTOMATIC EQUIPMENT

Automatic equipment is equipment that is power operated either by electricity or battery. This type of equipment is very expensive and must be properly maintained to insure good service and maximum efficiency. Therefore, keep this equipment free of dirt, and oiled properly, and keep screws and nuts tight. Automatic equipment is usually divided into three categories: floor machines, vacuum cleaners, and automatic scrubbers.

EQUIPMENT:
    Single disc floor machines, with or without spray attachments
    Drive assemblies
    Square buffers—attachments (plates and baseboard scrubbers)
    Shampoo machines
    Vacuums
        a. Suction
        b. Back-Pack
        c. Wet and dry
        d. Pile lifter
        e. Upright

Vacuum attachments (wand, hose, crevice tool, brushes), floor, wall, ceiling, upholstery, carpet and attachments for wet floor operation.
Battery-operated sweepers
Automatic mop assemblies

PROCEDURE

Floor Machines

1. Used for scrubbing, stripping, and polishing of large or small areas quickly. Also used for special application, such as spray buffing and dry stripping.
2. Never attach brush by running machine over it and allowing it to lock.
3. Never leave machine unattended. Disconnect when not in use.
4. Machine is cleaned at the end of the day or after completion of assignment.

    a. At the work site, tilt machine back on handle. Remove brush and pad or drive assembly and place in plastic liners/bags.
    b. Rinse machine in upright position. Damp wipe cord with germicidal cloth. Wind cord on handle or storage hooks as it is being wiped. Inspect for defects and report to supervisor.
    c. Take equipment to utility room. Remove brushes, pads and/or drive assembly from plastic liners/bags. Wash thoroughly under running water. Store on flat surface or hang on peg to dry. DO NOT USE AGAIN UNTIL DRY.
    d. Wash handle and exterior surface of machine. Dry.
    e. Tilt on handle and rinse the underside of the brush housing with clean water. Dry.
    f. If a solution tank is used, rinse tank and feed lines/tubing. Dry.
    g. Store equipment in designated storage area.
    h. Never store machines on brushes. Store in tilted position.

Extension Cords

1. If an extension cord is used, make sure it is the same size as on the equipment so that the proper amount of current is carried to machine.
2. Do not yank on an electric cord to pull the plug from the outlet.
3. Damp wipe cord with germicidal solution. Dry.
4. Wind loosely and hang or lay in a safe place.

Vacuum Cleaners (Upright, Wet and Dry, Back-Pack)

1. Used to remove soil from floors and carpeting, window sills, ledges, screens, vents, blinds, upholstery, walls, and ceiling; and to pick up water—scrub, rinse, overflow, flooding.
2. Empty upright vacuums when bag is half full
    a. Outer bags may be cloth, moleskin, or paper.
    b. Cloth and moleskin bags may be vacuumed, but never washed. Discard disposable bags.
    c. Damp wipe handle, hose, and cord with germicidal solution. Dry.
3. Clean wet and dry vacuum at the end of the day.
    a. If used for dry purposes:
        (1) Make sure machine is set up with flannel and paper liners.

(2) To clean, remove hose, head assembly, and cloth filter. Leave paper filter in place.
(3) Tilt machine back on handle and wheels. Pull out bag so that it hangs outward.
(4) Continue raising machine until it is resting on handle. Slap tank several times to dislodge all dirt.
(5) Remove bag by sliding elastic band off the lip of the tank. Place in a plastic liner. Tie and discard.
(6) Wash tank inside and outside with germicidal solution. Rinse and dry.
(7) Wash all attachments. Rinse and dry.
(8) Wipe off cord and rewind on handle, not around head assembly.
(9) Wipe off head assembly.
(10) Check impaction filter. Not necessary to remove after each usage, unless torn, damaged or wet. Supervisor should set a specific time for changing (for example, every 30 days).
(11) Take equipment to designated storage area. Leave head assembly off tank. Turn on side for airing and drying purposes.

  b. If used for wet purposes:
(1) Make sure machine is set up for the wet operation.
(2) Remove flannel and paper liners and insert the cyclonic separator which has a float that shuts off the suction of the machine when tank is filled to maximum level.
(3) To clean, remove hose, head assembly, and lift out cyclonic separator.
(4) Wheel machine to area with drain or low sink. Tilt back on handles to empty. (Some of these have drain valves.)
(5) Rinse two or three times with clean water to remove sludge.
(6) Wash, rinse, and dry tank and accessories.
(7) Store in designated storage area.
(8) If impaction filter is wet, allow to dry. Sterilize or autoclave before using again.

Automatic Scrubbers/Sweepers

Used for scrubbing, stripping, buffing, and sweeping large areas. In order for machines to work properly, they must be charged daily in a well-ventilated room. Battery must be checked regularly and distilled water added when water is below internal plate or triangle. Battery cover must be left opened when charging. Do not smoke in area when machine is being charged.

1. Automatic Scrubber
   a. To clean, take equipment to utility room. Empty; open dump valve or fold tanks over drain.
   b. Flush tanks, wheels, and squeegee. Use a hose to perform this task.
   c. Wash exterior surface with germicidal solution.
   d. Rinse and dry.
   e. Take to designated storage area.
   f. Make sure windows are open.
   g. Report any defects, damages, or necessary repairs to supervisor.

2. Powered Sweeper
   a. To clean, take to utility room. Remove and empty trash pan.
   b. Shake down filters; remove and empty pan.

c. Remove brushes; comb, wash, rinse, and shake well. Dry.
d. Wash exterior surface with germicidal solution. Rinse and dry.
e. Wash pans. Rinse and dry.
f. Replace all parts.
g. Take to designated storage area.
h. Check battery; leave cover open.
i. Connect for charging.
j. Make sure windows are open.
k. Report any defects or necessary repairs to supervisor

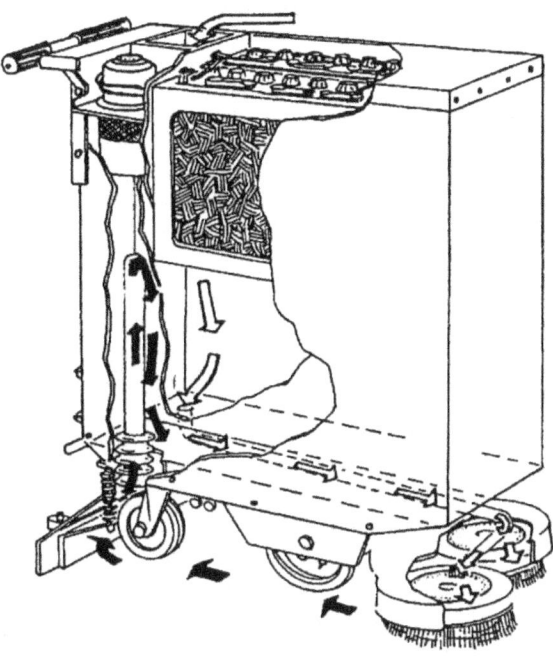
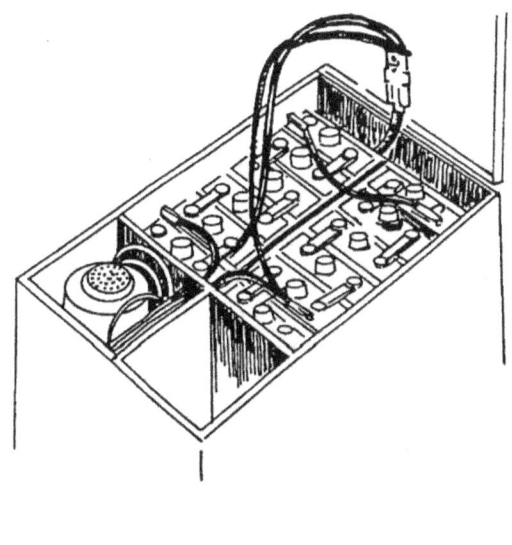

IV. HELPFUL SERVICE HINTS FOR WET AND DRY VACUUM

1. Always operate vacuum on the proper voltages as outlined on the data plate.

2. After using for dry applications, remove the disposable paper bag (5 to 9 gallon units only), and mitten flannel filter and clean before reusing. For added convenience, keep a supply of disposable paper bags on hand (5 and 9 gallon units only; they may be obtained from your authorized distributor.

3. If air movement is interrupted in your vacuum, check the dust filter to make sure it's clean. To see if hose has become clogged, remove hose from machine and test suction at machine intake. Sometimes a clogged tool will be the culprit, so check tools periodically.

4. For wet work, remove the disposable paper bag and dust filter, then place the water separator in the tank (5 and 9 gallon units only). In the 10 gallon models, install the wet filter and water shut-off.

5. After using machine for wet work, and before putting it away, clean tank inside and outside; clean tools thoroughly.

6. Store machinery in clean dry place.

7. The suds suppressor bar at the tank inlet should be checked and replaced, if necessary, after 125 gallons of solution have been picked up. Suds suppressor bar is replaced by removing inlet deflector and sliding new bar into place. These bars may be obtained from authorized distributor (for 5 and 9 gallon units only).

8. Many tools are available for the wet and dry vacuum. Contact your authorized distributor for additional tools.

SERVICE DIAGNOSIS:

1. Motor will not start
   a. Possible causes:
      (1) Power source or outlet dead
      (2) Vacuum switch faulty or damaged
      (3) Excessively worn brushes
      (4) Wire shorted or broken

   b. How to correct:
      (1) Activate source or check cord
      (2) Replace switch
      (3) Replace brushes
      (4) Replace wires

2. Little or no suction
   a. Possible causes:
      (1) Full tank; wet shut-off closes fan inlet
      (2) Clogged attachment inlet, hose or vacuum inlet
      (3) Clogged filter bag
      (4) Tank gasket seal leaks
      (5) Exhaust air outlet covered

   b. How to correct:
      (1) Empty tank
      (2) Remove lodged materials
      (3) Clean filter bag
      (4) Position seal properly
      (5) Remove obstruction

3. Machine noisy
   a. Possible causes:
      (1) Vibration or resonating of metal parts
      (2) Dirty filter

b. How to correct:
   (1) Secure all mountings firmly
   (2) Clean filter

4. Motor runs hot or smells warm
   a. Possible causes:
      (1) Motor cooling air intake or exhaust clogged
      (2) Motor overloaded with mist or suds
      (3) Dirty filter

   b. How to correct:
      (1) Clean air intake and exhaust passages
      (2) Empty tank; install new suds suppressor
      (3) Clean filter

V. HELPFUL SERVICE HINTS FOR FLOOR MACHINES

SERVICE DIAGNOSIS:

1. Machine wobbles; hard to control
   a. Possible causes:
      (1) Brush bristles distorted resulting in brush being uneven
      (2) Switch housing not tight on handle tube
      (3) Handle tube not connected firmly to machine hose
      (4) Pads or brushes worn unevenly

   b. How to correct:
      (1) If brush is new, soak in water for several hours; remove from water; shake off excess water; rest brush on flat surface on back with bristles pointing upward.
      (2) Tighten bolts securing housing to handle tube; tighten set screws. If housing is still loose, drill and tap new hole in housing, insert pointed set screw and tighten firmly.
      (3) Check all mounting bolts for tightness; insert washers for shims if necessary.
      (4) Replace with new pad or brush.

2. Motor will not run
   a. Possible causes:
      (1) Unplugged at wall
      (2) Unplugged between motor and handle cable.
      (3) Fuse blown or circuit breaker tripped
      (4) Cable wires severed
      (5) Switch burned out
      (6) Wires detached at switch
      (7) Motor burned out

   b. How to correct; follow these steps:
      (1) Visibly check all connections to be sure the plugs are securely plugged into the appropriate receptacle.
      (2) Check fuse or circuit breaker. Replace or reset if necessary.

- (3) Visibly and carefully check cable for wire breakage.
- (4) Unplug motor from handle cable and connect motor directly to wall receptacle through use of an adequate gauge extension cord (at least 14-2). CAUTION: Remove brush or pad holder from machine before plugging into power source.
- (5) If after #4 above motor does not operate, remove motor from machine and take it to your distributor, or an electrical repair station designated by your distributor for repairs.
- (6) If after #4 above does operate, the problem lies between the motor and the wall receptacle. Remove switch box cover plate and ascertain that al electrical connections are secure.
- (7) Remove cable from the terminals on the switch and replace with an extension cord (preferably 14-3) to determine if wires have been severed inside the cable.
- (8) Replace switch.

3. Runs hot
   a. Possible causes:
   - (1) Motor overloaded. Machine does not have sufficient power for the job. (Example: dry spray-buff cleaning with abrasive pad.)
   - (2) Air intake ducts clogged with dust and lint.

   b. How to correct:
   - (1) Secure the proper machine for the job or use the same machine with pads of less abrasive material.
   - (2) Remove drip cover and shroud. Use forced air to blow dust and lint from motor.

VI. HELPFUL SERVICE HINTS FOR AUTOMATIC SCRUBBERS

SERVICE DIAGNOSIS:

1. Motor will not start
   a. Possible causes:
   - (1) Battery charge condition very low; check with hydrometer
   - (2) Battery connectors loose or disconnected
   - (3) Loose or broken wires

   b. How to correct:
   - (1) Recharge batteries fully before beginning operations
   - (2) Fasten battery connections securely
   - (3) Fasten all wires securely and tape

2. Machine will not move
   a. Possible causes:
   - (1) Clutch requires adjusting
   - (2) "V" belt slipping
   - (3) Battery charge condition very low; check with hydrometer

b. How to correct:
   (1) Adjust clutch per "Clutch Adjustment" instructions
   (2) Adjust "V" belt tightness
   (3) Recharge batteries fully before beginning operations

3. Machine streaking a cleaned floor
   a. Possible causes:
      (1) Foreign materials lodged under rear squeegee blade
      (2) Insufficient water flow to brushes
      (3) Worn squeegee blades
      (4) Squeegee out of adjustment
      (5) Worn brushes or pads

   b. How to correct:
      (1) Raise squeegee and clean squeegee blade
      (2) Clean fine filter screen in tank and examine lines for a flow restriction
      (3) Replace squeegee blade
      (4) Adjust per instructions
      (5) Replace brushes or pads

4. Solution not being properly picked up
   a. Possible causes:
      (1) Vacuum motor wired for 12 or 18 volts and too much solution being laid
      (2) Clogged pick-up tube
      (3) Air leaks around vacuum motor mount
      (4) Ball check (water shut-off) sealing vacuum motor opening to tank
      (5) Clogged filters
      (6) Drain valve not completely closed
      (7) Pick-up tube plug or suds suppressors not seated properly

   b. How to correct:
      (1) Use 24-volt switch position
      (2) Remove lint accumulations and clean tube through plugged hole in tank at top of tube
      (3) Seal all leaks
      (4) Clean ball check (water shut-off) assembly
      (5) Replace filters
      (6) Close valve
      (7) Securely seat pick-up tube plug

5. Short operating time
   a. Possible causes:
      (1) Battery charge condition very low; check with hydrometer
      (2) Continuous heavy motor load due to special brushes
      (3) Constant brush operation; 210 lb. position

   b. How to correct:
      (1) Recharge batteries fully before beginning operations
      (2) Use special brushes requiring heavy motor load only for particular application
      (3) Use locked brush cleaning operations sparingly

6. Machine pulls to one side
    a. Possible causes
        (1) Squeegee dragging only on one side

    b. How to correct:
        (1) Adjust per instructions

7. Machine creeps
    a. Possible causes:
        (1) Clutch out of proper adjustment
        (2) Clutch cable binding in wound wire casing
        (3) Clutch collar sticking

    b. How to correct:
        (1) Adjust clutch per "Clutch Adjustment" instructions
        (2) Lubricate clutch cable and casing
        (3) Lubricate clutch

www.ingramcontent.com/pod-product-compliance
Lightning Source LLC
Chambersburg PA
CBHW081825300426
44116CB00014B/2485